Ron Arad
talks to Matthew Collings

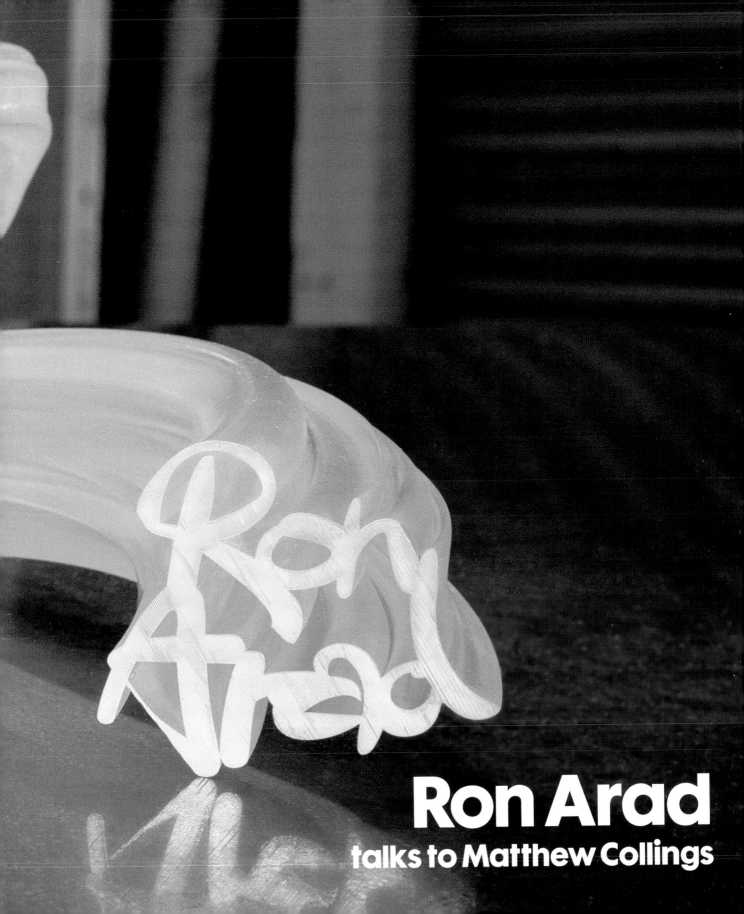

Ron Arad

talks to Matthew Collings

1

Difference between art and design
Yes to minimal
Different minimal
Documenta punch-up

Difference between art and design

Collings

What is design?

Arad

Well, if you ask me like that, I'd say that maybe design is the act of one imposing one's will on materials to perform a function.

Collings

That's a good definition. I wish I could be as clear about art.

Arad

According to Oscar Wilde, the element of function disqualifies something from being art. But actually an art form's function might be to entertain or delight: for example, Brian Eno flirted for a while with the idea of music being functional. He came up with things like music for airports, or for lifts.

Collings

I remember getting the message at art school that art was like music: 'art aspires to the condition of music'. It was a leftover cliché from Formalism. You get infected with all this information at art school without having any idea if it's still current. But its use when it was significant was that it supplied an explanation of abstract art's function, or an apology for why there wasn't one. And you could adapt it for the life studio just as well: the lovely daubs are more important in themselves than getting the eyelashes in the right place.

Arad

Function isn't the end of the story. Some people confuse function with being practical. You can make a chair that's totally impractical, but it's still a chair because it's about sitting. It's something you sit in, or sit on, but it might be too heavy to move, for example. Or it could be too cold to sit on. But at least to be called design it has to fulfil some necessary condition. On the other hand there's a whole history of people making chairs where the maker isn't a designer but an artist, like Scott Burton or Richard Artschwager. Or Roy Lichtenstein: you know, his 'brush stroke' chair.

Collings

I think of Richard Artschwager as an also-ran Pop artist, who did a lot of mock tables and chairs in Formica. Not as famous as the main Pop figures,

Left
New Orleans
Armchair
1999
Pigmented polyester reinforced with fibreglass
Edition of 18 unique pieces
Handmade by Ron for The Gallery Mourmans

'The New Orleans was moulded to the shape of the Big Easy. The series spent a very short amount of time in our studio, so our knowledge of these chairs is mainly based on memory, assisted by a few photographs.'

Below
Richard Artschwager
Table with Pink Tablecloth
1964
Formica-covered, table-size wooden block

but having a little second-time-around spurt of intellectual fashion buzz about him, in the late 1980s. And Scott Burton is a 1970s and 80s figure who, before he died of AIDS, had some success with crossover sculptures that – as I remember, although I never took much notice of them – combined something like a rock with a chair. I thought the point with both of them, as with Roy Lichtenstein's mock furniture, was that they all deliberately mucked about with an ordinary notion that people have of an eternal opposition between design and art.

Arad

Yes but with Scott Burton, I always thought his chairs weren't good enough as chairs or as art. He decided to play the art field, which means going to art openings – or making sure that when he exhibits his designs the place is closed on Mondays, because shops are open Mondays but art galleries are not. But really a lot of his chairs weren't a million miles away from what Rietveld did before him only better.

Collings

I feel I know when something is more design than art but I'm completely naïve about what design actually is, its history and so on. I could never be an authority on design! But I notice more and more that design is very visual, while art – which is assumed to be the highest realm of the visual – is becoming less and less so. Aesthetically it gets more and more kind of – nothing. Anyway, for most people, they don't care about philosophizing distinctions. They notice normal things like cost...

Arad

Yes – 'How much is this? How much is this? Ooh, so much – £10,000 for a chair! That's a lot'. You don't say that about a sculpture. Because people don't know how much a sculpture usually is. But a chair – they know. And they know you can get six for £100 or whatever. So cost brings the chair to a realm that people think they know.

Collings

I used to find Scott Burton boring but I thought, well, if I don't know about design, maybe what he does is just alien to me. So I didn't think any more about it.

Arad

Did it matter to you that you didn't know about design?

Collings

Not in those days. Now I'm embarrassed by it – I don't usually tell anyone.

Yes to minimal

Collings

Donald Judd did chairs, too. His chairs were functional but there's an aura of art about them, because of who did them and what they look like: they look like 1960s Minimalism, and they're done by the main figure of that

Above
Scott Burton
Rock Chair
1981
Bushnami Sculpture Garden, Burton, Texas

Below
Donald Judd
Chair
1991

movement. Do you think those chairs are good design?

Arad

He was very influential in the design world, in fact the whole Minimalist movement was.

Collings

You mean Judd's Minimalist Art was influential, his boxes and stacks, and so on – but not his chairs?

Arad

No, I mean his Minimalist Art was very influential and that includes his chairs. That Judd chair stripped down the idea of the chair: you know, something that is always 45cm off the ground, it supports itself, you can lean back in it to some extent…

Collings

It was impressive to strip it down?

Arad

Oh yes. The modern chair peaked in the 1950s with Eames, Nelson, Jacobsen, Prouvé, all these people that had a lot of things to rebel against. For our generation, yours and mine – well, we were left with nothing to rebel against, almost. Judd went a step further than the 1950s people, and stripped the chair of industrial sense, or industrial common sense. Stripped it of comfort, ergonomics, anything like that. And yet it answered the necessary condition to be a chair. Or in the case of his other design works, to be a piece of furniture, to be a table. But thinking of the chair alone: really, comfort is an illusion to a great degree. I know this from the Well Tempered Chair I did fifteen years ago. It was a piece of tempered steel I bent and then put together with wing nuts. When you looked at it you didn't think it was going to be comfortable. I made a video at the time of people's comments. They assumed it was going to be uncomfortable and then they'd sit in it and they'd be surprised, and say 'Actually, it's very comfortable'. And that's the telling thing, the fact that someone's expectation is contradicted, which in itself brings a certain type of pleasure and delight: expectation is broken in a positive way.

Collings

So comfort is mental habit as much as anything?

Arad

It's not what you expect, but most times people don't think things through. If the food is very good in a restaurant, you're not worried about the chairs. I mean, if they're comfortable or not: it's not the main issue. It's only when the chair becomes a subject itself, when people sit on one and they think the context somehow makes it absolutely necessary for them to have an opinion, at that point comfort becomes an issue. But Judd created a language and a whole ideology and philosophy. It was an aesthetic and in a way it was a religion, a very strict one at that. He had a great influence on anyone from John Pawson to Jasper Morrison to Claudio Silvestrin.

Above
Jean Prouvé
Standard Chair
1934
Vitra

Below
Arne Jacobsen
Egg Chair (left) and **Swan Chair**
1958
Fritz Hansen

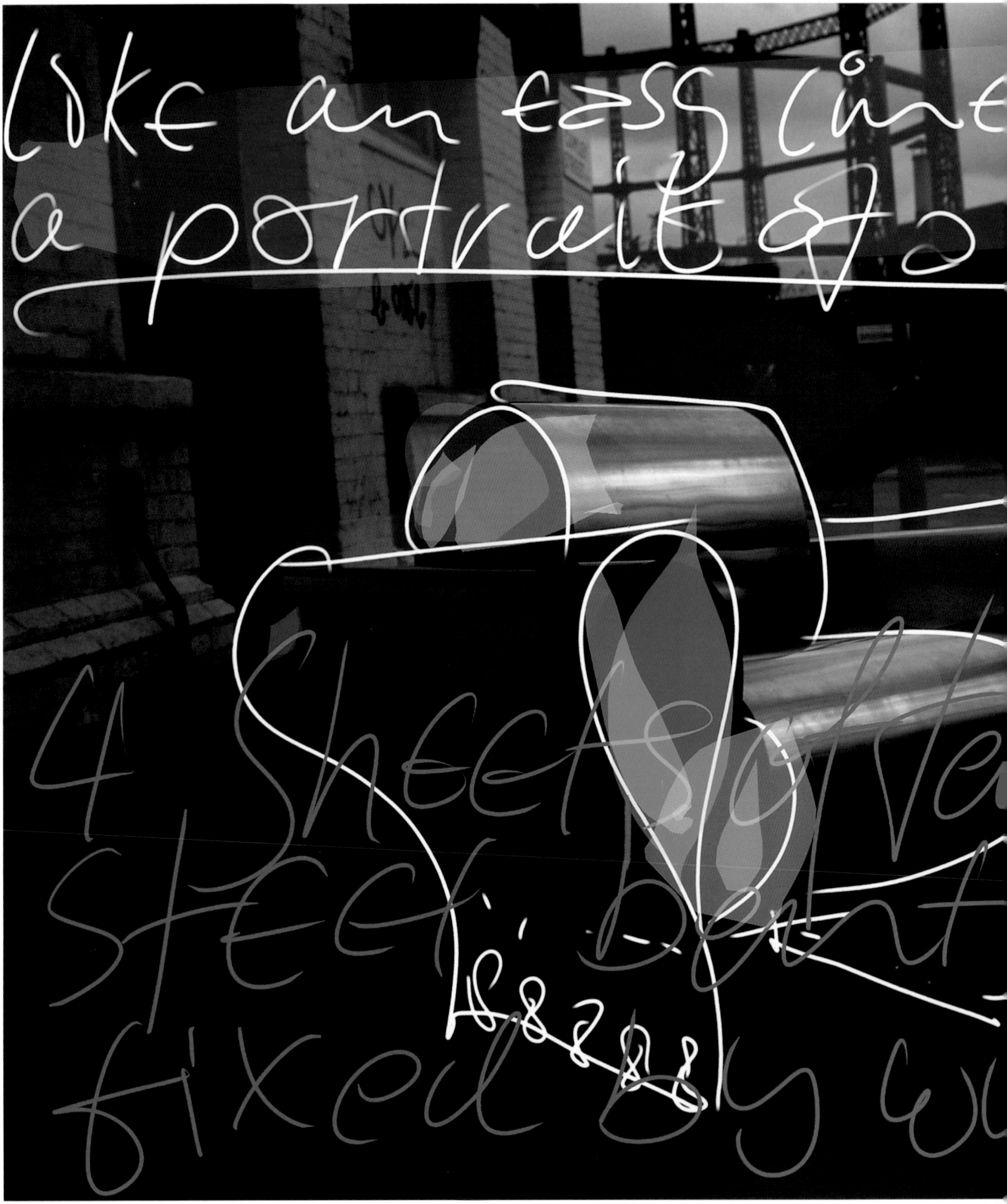

like an easy line
a portrait so

4 sheetsolve
steel bent
fixed by w

Well Tempered Chair
1986
Tempered stainless steel sheets, wing-nuts
Vitra Editions

Main image: an explanation of the thinking behind the Well Tempered Chair, this montage was produced for 'Taking Liberties', an exhibition of Ron's work held at the Centre Santa Monica, Barcelona in 2003.

first prototype of 'Red Tempered Chair'
an experiment in using a composite,
designed material to replicate the
behaviour of
tempered steel

use
wingnuts
like in the
"well tempered"
it is important
to show the reversibility
of the spring panels

seat,
back
& arms
designed to
different flexibility
by different directions
of fabric layers

the potential energy captured by the act
of bending tempered steel & sheets of carbon-
fibre.

first prototype of 'Bad.Pic'

Increase gap
between
arms & seat
to avoid
trapped
fingers

this line
should be
cut in a
parallel curve
(not square)

loose the
joint cue
by @ form seat
in one piece
or b) move cue back
A) side to avoid C. float

rubber
extrusions
possibly
c channels
or maybe
I section

B) side to get
own identity

And I think Minimalism in design is still the prevailing movement, if there is one today.

Different minimal

Collings

Minimalism in the 1980s means something different to an art-world notion of Minimalism. It was in the 80s that Minimalism first acquired the popular dimension it still has today: to be trendy in that decade you'd know something about Minimalism. If you had a bit of wealth as well as being trendy you'd have a minimalist flat. Another thing that happened then was that people started thinking about design as well. Design was a rarefied thing before, not popular. But in the 80s it became clever or amusing to notice it and talk about it. Even to be familiar with the names of some designers. Of course these are relative degrees of popularity I'm talking about. Minimalism isn't truly popular, or wholly popular, but it is part of lifestyle now.

Arad

Right, it's true that Judd's art was never about lifestyle. And Minimalism was an integral part of art world discourse, but that didn't stop it from being influential in the design world. And yes, the boundaries are blurry. They always are. It's difficult to explain to a layman why this chair here, a Judd, is art, while this chair here, a Rietveld, is design. The Rietveld has more colours, and it's called 'Red and Blue Chair' (although it has yellow), and actually it's more adventurous than the Judd. It's more sculptural, there's more form going into it. It's pretty austere and, yes, 'minimal': the straight planks, the separated pieces of wood. And yet, we've got to believe that one is art and one is design. Take them to the middle of Covent Garden and ask passers-by what they think. Then when they answer tell them, 'No, you are wrong'. If you tell them which is art and which is design, they'll think you're having them on – they'll think, why that distinction?

Documenta punch-up

Collings

You were in Documenta once, weren't you?

Arad

I had the pleasure of exhibiting in Documenta in 1986, when the organizer, Manfred Schneckenberger, decided to have art and design.

Collings

Right in the middle of the whole design popular revolution of the 80s...

Arad

Yes. In most cases the chairs that people like Philippe Starck exhibited in Documenta didn't look any different, to most Documenta visitors, than

Previous
Bad Tempered Chair
2002
Carbon fibre, wing-nuts
Vitra

Annotated work-in-progress photographs showing the first prototype of the Bad Tempered Chair, a reworking of the Well Tempered Chair. 'This remake slightly improved the patterns of the Well Tempered, but lost none of its essential simplicity and elasticity. Unlike the uniform flexibility you get from stainless steel, carbon fibre allowed us to control the flexibility – the chair is practically weightless.'

Gerrit Thomas Rietveld
Red and Blue Chair
1918
Cassina

any of the guards' chairs that the organizers would hire and put there anyway. I did something for the show that the artists in it were very fast to dismiss as mere design, and the designers were equally fast to dismiss as art. It was a little aluminium carpet that could be winched up to be two chairs and was called 'Full House'. Because I grew up in an art background rather than a design background, I always thought of Documenta as this mythical event: 'Oh, they invited me to exhibit there, oh!' Anyway, the same year the Corsican artist, Ange Leccia, was also invited. You know him?

Collings

Yeah, two cars pointing at each other with the headlights on: big then, forgotten now.

Arad

Well, in this case he showed a different work, a single car on a kind of turntable. He got Mercedes to provide their latest piece of design for the work, their latest car. So here was the latest Mercedes, a car hardly seen anywhere until then, slowly turning on this revolving plinth. And because the idea of the organizers was to mix design and art they also wanted to have Alessandro Mendini exhibiting nearby. Mendini's a designer, a sort of veteran shaman-figure or guru, from the avant-garde of Italian designers. He started out with Alchimia, and he was on the fringes of Memphis. Anyway, Mendini decided to put in some paintings. He was a designer but he wanted to show paintings: these hard edge black and yellow paintings, with sort of patterns. And Leccia said, 'I'm not having design in my room'. And they told him, 'Sorry, this is what we have decided to do'. And it developed into a serious physical fight. The artist wanted to show some design, and the designer wanted to show some art. And the artist says, 'I'm not having design in my room'.

Collings

There was an idea in the international art world in the mid-80s of the rise of design within an art context, as a dangerous or creatively subversive notion. It was supposed to be a challenge to subjectivity, which was represented by Neo-Expressionist painting: the Neo-Expressionists were 'subjective', and the model-makers (which was a name for the German version of this new design-and-architecture oriented sculpture) were 'objective'. There were all sorts of angles on it. You'd get jokey hip German artists like Martin Kippenberger introducing a design element in order partly to attack this model-maker artist, Reinhard Mucha, say, a much more solemn figure, who'd had a lot of success because of a design-look to his sculptures. Kippenberger had previously done a bit of satirizing of Neo-Expressionism, but now he was satirizing this design fad. I remember others in the Kippenberger circle were impressed by the seriousness with which Mucha was taken by the power sections of the art world, then. And they'd refer to Mucha's look as 'designer-Beuys', meaning a shallow people-pleasing version of something that ought to be

Full House
Chairs
1986
Aluminium, stainless-steel wire hinges
Edition of 1
One Off

Above: a preliminary sketch for Full House. This chair design was produced for Documenta 8, held in Kassel in 1986. Below: Full House in situ at Documenta.

Left
Looploop
Chair
1992
Woven and polished stainless steel, mild-steel
Edition of 5
One Off

'The material we used is similar to that developed for making conveyor belts in the food industry. The chair is formed by binding two structural profiles together with a metal fabric that follows their outlines.'

Above
Liam Gillick
Installation for the Turner Prize
Tate Britain, London
2002

Below
Peter Halley
Sylvester
1991

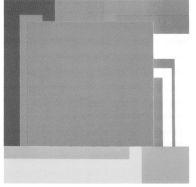

deep or difficult. And then you had the New York Neo-Geo artists, Jeff Koons, Peter Halley, Ashley Bickerton and Haim Steinbach, coming from a different angle on design: all rising as superstars at this time, and all presenting this gleaming glamorous shiny object kind of look. The look said, 'Fuck you' to Neo Expressionist painting, and it really killed off that particular painting trend. But it wasn't just the attack on painting that made this design-fascination significant, it was the introduction of a sophisticated idea about the realm of 'the social' that design or architecture was supposed to stand for, and that art now wanted to get involved in. It made it possible for a figure like Dan Graham, who'd been forgotten, from the old Conceptual-Minimal days of the 1960s and 70s, to re-emerge as a god. And the legacy of that mid-1980s moment today is Liam Gillick in the Turner Prize. But now what makes me smile is that you're describing almost a satirical cartoon, but in real life: an art person and a designer person beating each other up.

Arad

Well, actually it wasn't the artist and the designer, it was the organizer and the artist...

Collings

But they were fighting over an issue of art and design?

Arad

Right. It was beautiful. I wouldn't have missed it for anything, this art and design Documenta – the whole thing was funny. In the cafeteria you never saw designers and artists mixing.

Collings

Really?

Arad

Absolutely – the exhibition was supposed to be the great attempt to bridge the gap but what it did it was...

Collings

Consolidate the gap even more?

Arad

Yeah. It just proved they're oil and water, although I don't think it set out to represent that.

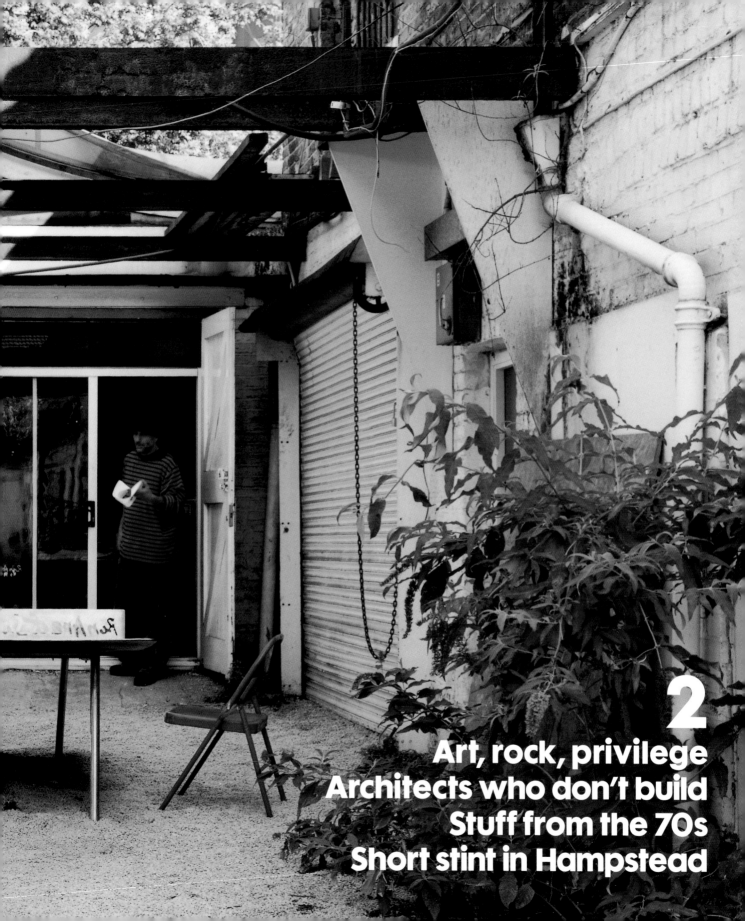

2
Art, rock, privilege
Architects who don't build
Stuff from the 70s
Short stint in Hampstead

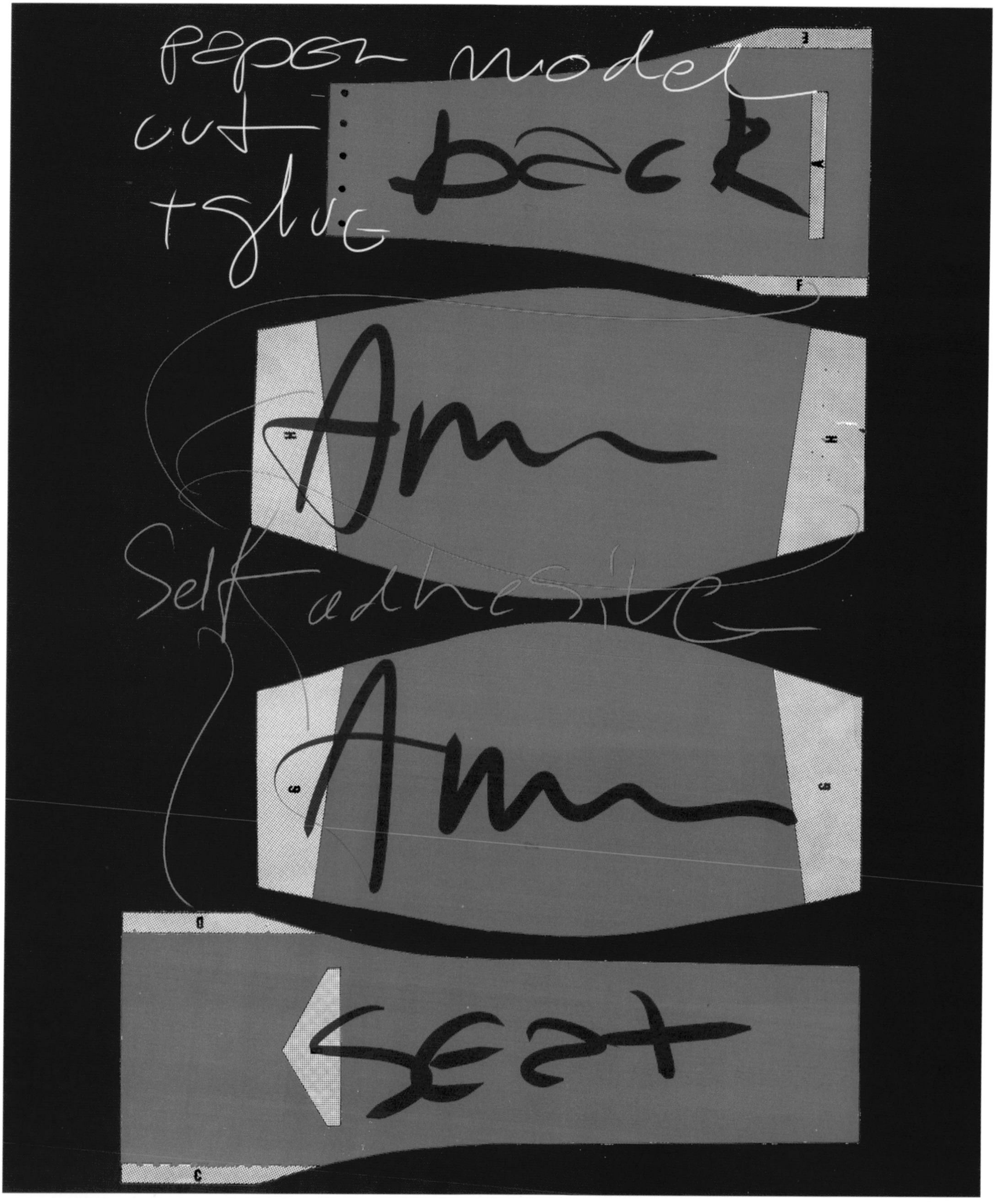

paper model
cut
+glue

back

self adhesive

Am

Am

seat

Art, rock, privilege

Collings

You mentioned you grew up in an art background. What were the stages going from art into design?

Arad

I grew up when Pop was important. I wanted to draw like Claes Oldenburg. There are books where he has all these pencil drawings, and I'd look at them and think, 'This is drawing!' And they all depicted things. There was an amazing book published by the Ludwig Museum in Cologne, this museum mostly of Pop Art, as it was in those days. I think it was a catalogue of their Pop collection, but it was an amazing work of design. People talk about the magic of LP covers, the way teenagers invent themselves in relation to these illuminated icons. For me, that book was the equivalent. At that time I wasn't sure if Oldenburg was the thing, or Dylan. But that book was my window from the margin to the centre, from Tel Aviv out to wherever the centre was supposed to be. I looked at it intensely. And I had a subscription for Artforum from the age of sixteen. From a distance, you take things much more seriously. When I speak to people now in Tel Aviv, I can still tell how accidental their information is. So here I was, a spoilt brat, but at the same time, because of these things I absorbed, I grew up with an acute aversion to convention: it was all against the tide, against the mainstream.

Collings

You were excited by art when you were young, but the particular type of art had a stylish, modern look to it?

Arad

Yeah, it did. I regretted not going to the Blue Mountain College, or whatever.

Collings

With John Cage and Rauschenberg, and so on – the legendary figures behind the Pop Art world?

Arad

Yes. I thought, 'This is where it all happened'.

Collings

Black Mountain College.

Arad

Did I say blue? Black Mountain, yes. Anyway, at the same time I regretted not being Dylan. When people stick a microphone in front of your face and say, 'What are your greatest influences?', if I'm true to myself, I have to say Dylan.

Collings

But maybe rock culture and modern art culture were equally hypnotic?

Left

Well Tempered Chair

Patterns for a 'make-it-yourself' paper model of the chair
1986

The Spanish design magazine, Ardi, included this scale model in one of its first issues. 'Use this page – maybe a photocopy is best – to make your own Well Tempered Chair.'

Below

Art of the Sixties

1971
The Wallraf-Richartz Museum and the Ludwig Foundation, Cologne

Made up of sections comprising image-printed acetate sheets, a variety of paper stocks and hand-stuck printed images, and bound using nuts, bolts, PVC and hard-case plastic, this rare book catalogues the work of 92 artists.

Above
Esther Perez-Arad (Ron's mother)
Untitled
1949

Below
Grisha Arad (Ron's father)
Hagar & Ishmail
1949

Arad

Yeah, and privileged culture. I do come from a very privileged background. There was art at home in Tel Aviv, there was music at home and there was respect for anything avant garde at home. But I never thought I was going to be a designer or an architect. Although every time I had a pencil in my hand, and I could do portraits of people that looked like them and I could draw, I mean, according to my mother, I was talented and gifted at drawing. So every time I did a fantastic drawing, at least it was fantastic in the family mythology. Or fantastic in the supportive parents sort of language: 'Ah, he's going to be an architect!' I never heard, 'He's going to be an artist'. I think there was actually a fear that I might want to become an artist, that I was certainly lazy enough to want to be one.

Collings

Why, because your mother was already an artist?

Arad

Both of them were.

Collings

They thought, 'There are enough artists in the family, let's have someone who can earn some money'?

Arad

Not to earn some money, so much – as well as being an artist, my father always had a daytime job that he felt was slavery. And consequently there's something in the culture of my family that sees something good in artistic tendencies, but they want them combined with something sound, as architecture is. Social responsibilities, common sense: those things as well should be in the picture, not just art.

Collings

So here you were on the outside looking in. You had an arty family, and you knew of this whole other world of fashionable happenings – you knew it from the media. Did you get all those films in Tel Aviv, did you know Darling and Morgan, and Blow Up, and so on?

Arad

Morgan is my favourite film of all time – David Warner. And the writer of that film, David Mercer – I said, 'Who is this David Mercer? What else did he do?' And also when you grow up on the periphery, it's as if every meaning gets amplified. I thought I knew everything about art from my bloody Artforum subscription. Later, when I went to the AA (Architectural Association) in London, I thought everyone there was ignorant.

Collings

You thought they'd all know about Robert Morris and Robert Smithson?

Arad

Not only that – I told this guy there that his drawings reminded me a lot of Kokoschka's drawings of the Thames, and he said, 'Hey! Who's Kokoschka?' It's funny, when I think of Penny Lane now, it doesn't remind me of Liverpool but Tel Aviv. And when I talk about this now, I think of meaning being distorted – as it was for me. I mean, I thought the 'meter maid' in Lovely Rita was someone a metre tall. I never knew what a meter maid was. I knew 'parking meter' appears in Dylan, too. There was a Lynn Chadwick sculpture in Jerusalem: I assumed Lynn Chadwick was a woman. So I sucked in every word from Artforum and from Dylan – I had to take him in, too. And I had to carefully listen to the three minutes of silence of John Cage: I mean, I had to. So I came to London because I had an image of London that is sort of based on something, but it of course wasn't really there.

Architects who don't build

Collings

Did you come to London especially to study at the Architectural Association?

Arad

No, absolutely not – it was 1973 and I came to give myself a break from a war zone. But I visited the AA and they were doing interviews, and I knew some people there, and it looked like a very exciting place...

Collings

Was the AA trendy then?

Arad

Very – you mentioned Blow Up, do you remember the virtual tennis game in that? They were all AA students: a crowd of jolly people in convertibles, going to a tennis court in a park. And then two of them play tennis without a ball, the 'ball' goes over the fence, and they're waiting for some other people who aren't part of the crowd, to fetch it...It was the heyday of conceptual art. At the Slade then they had typewriters. I went to the Slade, I went to the Royal College and I went to all these places you hear about. And the AA looked like fun to me. There were people experimenting with space there, experimenting with LSD...

Collings

... inner and outer space?

Arad

Yeah. I looked at it and thought, 'This is something!' And at that time, no one did any actual building: if they did, they had to apologize.

Collings

They just did concepts?

Arad

Yeah. This Swiss figure, Bernard Tschumi – nowadays he wants to build, but at the time I was at the AA everything he did was about ideas. Rosalee Goldberg, she wrote this book about Performance Art – do you remember her?

Above
Morgan: A Suitable Case for Treatment
1966
Film directed by Karel Reisz, written by David Mercer, starring Vanessa Redgrave and David Warner

Below
Blow Up
1966
Film directed and written by Michelangelo Antonioni, starring David Hemmings and Vanessa Redgrave

Collings

I know that book, yes.

Arad

Well she was Tschumi's partner, and Tschumi was an influential figure at the AA then. The parties at the AA were better than anyone else's parties. Remember, this was just my impression from visiting, it was before I was a student there. But anyway, one day they were interviewing people and I didn't plan to come for an interview: I didn't plan to become an architect at all. But I went anyway, and they asked, 'Can we see your portfolio?' And I said, 'Well, I don't have one. I have my 6B pencil. Do you want me to draw something for you?' I couldn't care less whether I got in or not. 'Why do you want to be an architect?' 'I don't want to be an architect. My mother would love me to be an architect but...' And so on and so forth.

Collings

So you had a bit of attitude, which they liked?

Arad

Yeah. It was the day of the election I remember: Labour got in.

Collings

1974, I suppose it must have been – April? I was working on a building site in Victoria, waiting to start art school later in the year.

Arad

Good, did you finish the building on time? Anyway, on the day of this interview there'd been a party. You know: 'Let's watch the election on television'. In those days that didn't mean big screens, it was a black and white set in the bar. So I went to watch the results, and someone from the panel which had interviewed me earlier came up to me in there and said, 'Congratulations. We offered you a place – but don't do that again! It was a hard battle. This time you got away with it'. 'Ah, good', I said.

Collings

And then what happened?

Arad

I wasted three years at the AA.

Collings

How: playing, mucking about?

Bernard Tschumi
The Manhattan transcripts
1981

'Bernard's architectural drawings were about anything but buildings.'

1

2

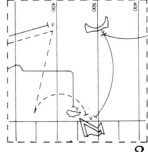

3

Mark Fisher
The Wall 80-10
1980

Installation at Earls Court stadium, designed for
Pink Floyd's The Wall tour

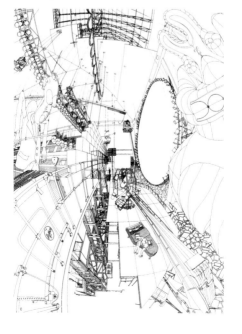

Arad

Well, showing what I could do. What I was better than them at. Which was drawing. They were struggling with drawings that I could easily do.

Collings

You had your facility for drawing...

Arad

Yeah, and a facility for bullshitting, as well. So I didn't learn anything. I was just there surviving on sandwiches I brought from home each day. It was partly a waste of time but partly not. The first part of the first year was all about competitions. There was this guy there called Mark Fisher, a very bright guy, very clever, who later got out of architecture to design all the sets for Pink Floyd's The Wall. He did a kind of rock and roll architecture. And after the first term, Mark said, 'Ron, you won all the competitions, you can draw better than everyone else – do you want to move to second year?' I said, 'Yes, please'. But that 'yes please' meant a lot of money for my parents, the fees were a strain on them.

Collings

You didn't have a scholarship or grant or anything?

Arad

No, they had to pay. In fact they wanted to pay for me. But in any case I moved up to the second year and I had a great time. Before, I wasn't interested in the AA or in architecture. I was elsewhere, I was a hippie. I was more interested in other stuff, in music: I thought music was much more important. But I got away with being elsewhere, and in fact it was easy to get away with it. And then when I moved to the diploma part, which is the final two years, I got hooked on architecture. And the reason for that was the presence of Tschumi – here was someone I could talk to about art. But also, there were others who were exciting like that: for example, Peter Cook, from Archigram.

Collings

They showed you a purpose?

Arad

They recognized me, I think. They never dreamed of ever building anything, and because of that they shifted the architectural debate away from building. I mean, they were all architects, committed architects, and they still are. The only thing in the world for them is architecture and architectural gossip: nothing else...

Collings

But at that time there was a conceptual purity to their architecture ideas?

Arad

Yeah. We thought at that time that architectural drawings were more important than building. That was their take, anyway, and something about me fitted with what they were into. I never saw myself spending years doing designs of offices, in a corduroy jacket. And the AA at this time, because of the ethos of these people, offered me an alternative. You didn't have to be an architect. There are no restrictions. Do what you like. This culture meant that they could not only tolerate anything but also appropriate anything. They felt that students like me enhanced their case. They needed people like me that could do things that they could publish, they could talk about – and they could show that this is fertile ground.

Collings

How did you change?

Arad

I felt good at the AA for the first time. I felt like I made a mark. I suppose it was exactly what I want my students now to feel: to feel good. To feel like they're the bee's knees. Maybe they could be the next big thing. But before that, there was a risk that I wanted to drop out and not get sucked into doing things like roof-slopes for the snow and rain, and drainage, and gutter and window details, and all this boring stuff.

Collings

And it was when you thought that what was inside you could have an outside correlate that you started to get excited, and that was shown to you by these people you came across, in the second year at the AA?

Arad

People like Tschumi and Cook, yeah. Cook was part of this very important group, Archigram – there were six of them altogether. Two others are dead now. And they were all friends of Eduardo Paolozzi: they did a kind of science-fiction thing. They had day jobs. They put out a magazine, also called Archigram. They never built anything. They came up with the idea of 'The Walking City', it was very influential, and it's still well known. It's just an idea, a proposal – a series of images. But it had a buzz of excitement and modernity around it, something like the equivalent of Richard Hamilton's picture, Just What Is It That Makes Today's Homes...– you know, it summed up the age, and it was a kind of criticism of the age, in a very inspired way. The other day the Archigram people were awarded the RIBA Gold Medal, that means they're up there now with Le Corbusier and Lloyd Wright.

Collings

Who else was there?

Arad

Nigel Coates, who later had the Nato group, was two years ahead of me at the AA, and he was my tutor for a year – it was Tschumi who brought Nigel into the AA. And there was Peter Wilson, a very clever designer and very good draftsman. And Rem Koolhaas: Koolhaas taught Zaha Hadid, who was in the next year above me. Koolhaas was an amazing lecturer and teacher. He had his book at this time, Delirious New York, and he gave a series of lectures on Coney Island. He was drawing Neo-Russian Constructivist architecture, which is still there, in a way: I mean you can see the genes of it in Zaha's work today, and in Koolhaas's work of today. Also, we had these easy-listening lectures from Charles Jencks, which were very important. I mean they were easy-listening because they really were very pleasurable experiences: he told anecdotes and stories about contemporary architecture. It was him who invented the term 'post-modern'.

Collings

So these glamorous names we hear about from time to time, the main lights of modern architecture: Koolhaas, and so on, these were your peers at the AA?

Arad

Slightly older peers, yes. They showed me there's some excitement to this world of architecture, it's not just a profession: there's some optimism, ambition – some arrogance. You need that. You know, the AA was really a pluralist place, the most radical, decadent place. Peter Cook described it well at RIBA the other day, at the Gold Medal event. He said it was young people working on abortive projects: it didn't matter what the project was, they knew it would be abortive. But if it was an ethos of pluralism at the AA, it was a kind of poker-faced pluralism. The director never showed his colours, he disliked everything in the same way! He was snide about everything in exactly the same measure. And that was fun, you realized it really was a broad church, after all, a container for everything. And in effect he really supported lots of stuff that might have been beyond his usual understanding.

Stuff from the 7Os

Collings

You eventually became hooked on architecture at the AA. What was the turning point for you, in terms of your own work?

Arad

I think it was entering a competition in 1978 to design a contemporary art museum for Aachen, in Germany. With this I thought I could accommodate a world that I'd been neglecting, which was contemporary art. At that time we were very excited about the idea that art is anything that invites you to look at it as art, and now I thought this could be translated into a building that housed art. It's funny, because you were dealing with a physical building that was going to emerge from half-baked thoughts about definitions of art, as if that kind of thing was actually important, and much less from practical or helpful ideas about how to light exhibitions, or something. Of course I was still only a student and it was only a competition, the building was never going to be built. So that was the AA and then there was the crash: what do you do after you graduate?

Collings

Hang on though, did you graduate with flying colours or what?

Peter Cook
Plug-in City
1964

'Peter had an amazing ability to master enthusiasm for any newness in architectural drawing – whether by his students or his contemporaries.'

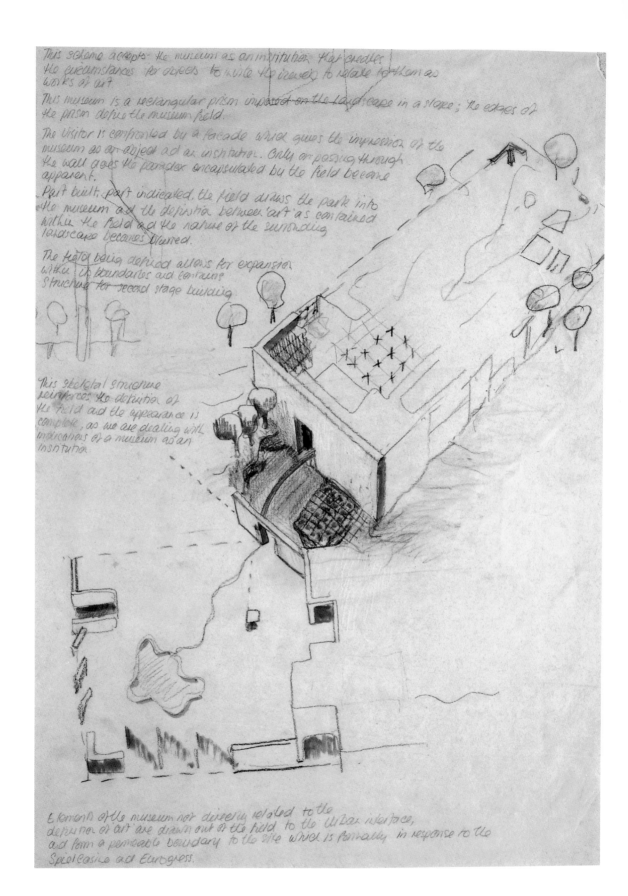

This scheme accepts the museum as an institution that creates
the circumstances for objects to incite the viewer to relate to them as
works of art.

This museum is a rectangular prism imposed on the landscape in a slope; the edges of
the prism define the museum field.

The visitor is confronted by a facade which gives the impression of the
museum as an object and an institution. Only on passing through
the wall does the paradox encapsulated by the field become
apparent.

Part built, part indicated, the field draws the park into
the museum and the definition between 'art' as contained
within the field and the nature of the surrounding
landscape becomes blurred.

The field being defined allows for expansion
within its boundaries and contains
structure for second stage building.

This skeletal structure
reinforces the definition of
the field and the appearance is
complete, as we are dealing with
indications of a museum as an
institution.

Elements of the museum not directly related to the
definition of art are drawn out of the field to the urban interface,
and form a permeable boundary to the site which is partially, in response to the
Spiel casino and Europress.

Left
Competition to design a contemporary art museum in Aachen, Germany
Sketch
1978

'This was part of my final-year project at the Architectural Association. It was only in my last year there that I started considering buildings, rather than architectural drawings, as the final product – as carriers of concepts.'

Right
Design for a prison in Soho, London
Sketch
1978

'My earlier architectural drawings were never conceived of as the blueprint of an actual building. The prison is an example of when an unlikely narrative – a prison in the middle of a city – can trigger architecture.'

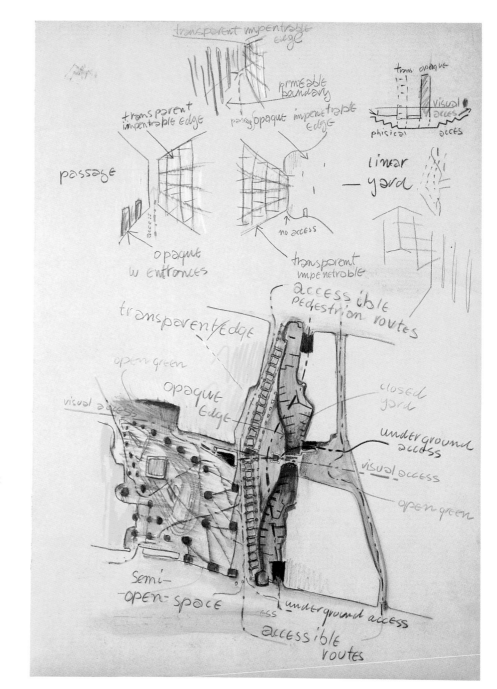

Arad

Oh yes.

Collings

What did you show?

Arad

I designed a kind of false-perspective stadium in Soho. It was a very wordy, heady project. It was supposed to be a public place which, when you look at it from a certain direction, it has a false-perspective stadium. That is, it's not real, it's a kind of trompe-l'oeil thing in the middle of Soho. It's a piece of urban architecture in a public space that pretends it could be built, and it can be used for anything – except maybe a stadium! But at the time I wanted make a place that would 'amplify' people, anyone who walked through there would appear to be big. There are precedents in classic theatre design: the auditorium continues the perspective of the stage, so if you're at the back or at the side, there's a place where the look is just right. It's hard to explain now why it seemed exciting. When Bernard calls me from New York nowadays he'll often say about something I've done: 'Oh, it's good to see the extension of your Soho stadium'.

Collings

What else did you do?

Arad

A project called 'Traffic Island'.

Collings

Like the J.G. Ballard story, Concrete Island? The man who lives on a traffic island, because he breaks down there, and he can't get off the motorway?

Arad

I don't know! It was an idea for Two Tree Island near Southend. That was the site we were given. The brief was, 'How would you use it? What would you do? So I did this science-fiction utopian-dystopian thing. The whole thing was about the fact that this was one of the most dense and terrible places to live. So in the project, you move slowly through the places where there are acres of open land around one house, and then it all changes as the social level changes, and the space. There were all sorts of jokes: the aerial view of the school for example looked like a hammer and sickle. And it was all drawn in this very stylish way, that loose, Oldenburg look.

Collings

But all these projects were only fantasies, everything everyone did then– they'd never be built? That was the spirit of the AA in the early-to-mid 1970s?

Arad

Yes true, but then again would the Pompidou Centre be possible without Archigram? Richard Rogers and Renzo Piano designed the Pompidou Centre, but it's an extension of Archigram and Peter Cook.

Drawing of a false-perspective stadium for a site in Soho, London

1978

Design for a Traffic Island
1978
Drawing

'This was me blending architecture and science
fiction in my early days at the Architectural
Association. It was like doing architecture with
the narrative of a comic strip.'

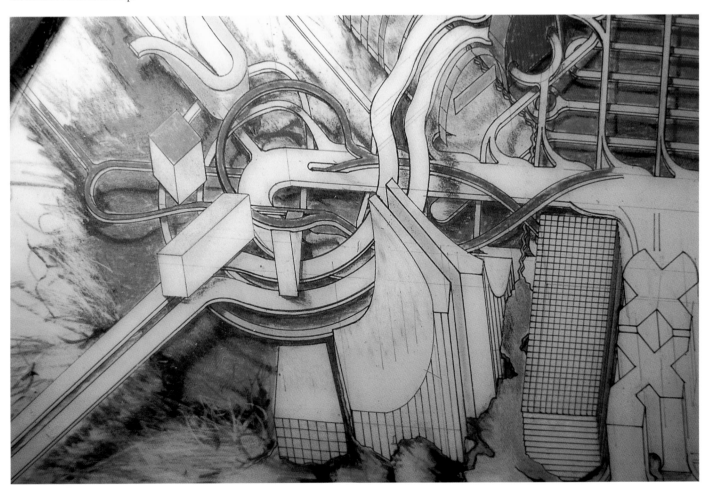

Short stint in Hampstead

Collings

So it was 1979, you'd left the AA – what happened?

Arad

I did what people normally do who've just left the AA, which is to work in someone else's practice. And this is the biggest crash you can ever experience. To work for other people, it's so...and even more so after lunch! And the fact is, one lunchtime I said, 'Fuck it. I'm not going back'. It was a practice in Hampstead. I just said, 'I'm not doing that now. This is not what I trained myself to do. This is not what I want to do'.

Collings

What about your wages?

Arad

I never had anxiety about where the bread would be coming from, because, well, I don't know – I felt I could always support myself somehow. I never had that fear or hunger or whatever that leads to that kind of existential anxiety. As I said, I was privileged. And I'd read Marcel Duchamp's biography: the beginning bit where he says he never had to worry about money.

Collings

So technically you might have had to worry about money a bit, but psychologically you felt protected because you'd been brought up feeling protected?

Arad

Of course technically I did have to worry about it and I still do, because now we have to pay twelve people's wages.

Collings

And it could all go wrong any day.

Arad

It could but I'm not worried about it. I might ask Caroline, my partner at the studio, 'Do we have money in the bank? Did we get royalties from so-and-so...?' 'Don't worry – it's OK.' You know, I've never written a cheque in my life. Well, almost not. Or opened an invoice. I'm lucky.

Collings

I can't believe you've never written a cheque.

Arad

Almost not – I know if I were growing up today, they'd have corrected me.

Collings

Yes, it's a very different time.

Arad

They would have spotted my problem.

3
Rover Chair, Covent Garden
DIY, scaffolding, surviving
Public's unexpected lust for design
Parties
Publicity, VAT, the Home Office
More stuff in boom climate

Rover chair, Covent Garden

Collings

You were out of the architectural practice, it was the beginning of the 80s and you didn't know what to do...

Arad

And I had no idea about design or about furniture or about anything. But I found a studio in Covent Garden near the Acme Gallery – do you remember that place?

Collings

Yes, of course.

Arad

And do you remember the big hole near it?

Collings

Yes, totally. It was a big hole where they were building what we now call Covent Garden. It was a shabby old building site, with boards round it.

Arad

Well, I went for a walk round there and I saw a shutter, and I looked in and there was a big butterfly in there, kind of a prop for something, I assumed. And there was, a little driveway, and I wondered to myself, 'What's happening here? – Ah, it belongs to the GLC'. I wandered down the driveway to a theatre props shop and asked, 'Who uses it?'. 'We use it sometimes' I was told. ' We do some props, like the ones in the back of the alley'. 'Oh, what do you mean sometimes?' 'Well, only when we have to do big things, like this butterfly'. 'Can I use it the rest of the time?' 'Sure'. I didn't have the faintest idea what I was going to do in it. But it had a shutter that you could lift, and there was a myth that it had been a place where they'd stored elephants at some time. It was some circus, or something. So I shared this place with a props maker whose boyfriend was a high ranking guy at the GLC, and after a while he just said, 'Ok, it's yours.' And so it was

One Off's studio/workshop in Shorts Gardens, Covent Garden

1981

'The place in Shorts Gardens was a great first home for One Off, although we had a serious wasp problem! In this picture, you can see our first-ever Rover Chair, a 'hi-tech' four-poster bed, a prototype of the Rocking Chair, and in the foreground, some old bus doors we got from London Transport.'

my studio. And of course Covent Garden was an exotic place at the time – it was 1980.

Collings

Yes, that was the time of Ken Livingstone, wasn't it? When the bus fares suddenly only cost 2p, because he brought them all down. And then they had to go back up again because it was unreal! I'd just started working at an art magazine then, in a little office in Dryden Street, sharing with a modern dance outfit. And the Acme Gallery was considered to be very impressive, very on the ball.

Arad

It was when Stuart Brisley...

Collings

...sat around one Christmas in the gallery, with a Christmas dinner rotting on a table before him. He was starving himself for Christmas. You could go in and interrogate him as he went greyer and greyer. He'd croak out some responses. I remember at the same time this other guy being famous for banging his head in a tray of wet clay and then he'd exhibit the impression. Maybe that wasn't at Acme. There was a guy called Peter McLennon, I think, who walked in a little circle at Acme, naked, with a kipper tied to his head, or his cock, or something. It's funny now to think of you round the corner, then, about to ride the 80s design boom, or to start it. So what did you think you were going to do there?

Arad

I didn't know. I certainly didn't think about design. But the first thing I actually did was my first ever piece of furniture, which was the Rover Chair.

Collings

Did someone ask you to do it?

Arad

No. I just noticed there was so much design and engineering and craftsmanship in this leather car seat, and you'd see hundreds of them rotting in scrap-yards, and they're more comfortable than any chair you can buy in...where? I didn't even know where, because I didn't have any connection with the furniture world.

Collings

What was the point of having an idea about a chair if no one had asked you to have it? Was that common? Did you know that people did that? Did you know other designers who did that, who had ideas and no one had asked them?

Arad

No. I didn't know what designers did or how they carried on. I just thought I'd start doing things, so I did. I discovered scaffolding. I found out it was invented in 1932 by someone called Gasgoigne, for use in cowsheds to make these structures for milking the cows – kind of milking parlours. So I did some things with tubes and clamps and so on, and the first thing

Rover Chair
1981
Upholstered leather original Rover 2-litre car seat, tubular steel, Kee-Klamps
Several hundred (no record was kept)
One Off

'Although the piece was a readymade, this drawing (my favourite) was still the prime source of the piece's design.'

I did was this chair, the Rover Chair. I knew, like Duchamp, that you set a blind date with an object. And I knew it's not enough to say 'a car seat'. You have to say which car seat. I made my little research, and the funny thing is the scrapyard I went to is the one that's still round the back of the Round House across the road from where we're talking now, where my studio is, in Chalk Farm Road.

Collings

It's a car park now, isn't it, the scrapyard?

Arad

Both, a car park and a scrapyard. I went and looked and sniffed around, and there was a Greek guy there, and I bought two red leather seats off of him. They were out of a Rover. I had to dismantle them myself. They were leather and in perfect condition. They cost £29 each. And I thought, 'Wow! Have I really spent £29? Well go on then, do something with them'. So, I

90° In The Shade
Table
1991
Stainless steel, acrylic strips
Edition of 1
One Off

'This is Rachel Reynolds and Matt Stanwix welding and polishing 90° In The Shade, a table so big that it took years to find a home.'

made the frame, which was a semi-circle, and I put the things together that needed to be put together, and it was right first time. It didn't need to be improved. It was just: click! I made two and I had them in the Covent Garden studio.

Collings

How did the chairs go from a little funky DIY thing that's of interest only to you, to a desirable object that everyone wants?

Arad

Well, the first chairs were red. We had no idea that it's not very common, that red leather is rare. Indeed, now in auctions a red Rover Chair is twice as much as a black Rover. So my first ones were red, but nothing sold. But then this guy, this friend of a friend, is knocking on my door on Boxing Day

One Off's Studio/showroom in Shelton Street, Covent Garden

1996
Welded interiors

'The miles and miles of welding were a real initiation course for me and our team. We made the "light tattoos" by burning holes in the steel blocking on the windows with an oxyacetylene torch.'

in 1981. I told him, 'Sorry, we are closed'. He says, 'But I want to buy these chairs'. And it was Jean Paul Gaultier. I didn't know that, though, because I didn't know him. I just saw a nice little French man and he bought six and gave me the payment in full, right there, in cash – they were £99 each in those days. And after that, somehow, by some secret message on the radar or the tom-toms, or something, people couldn't get enough of Rover Chairs. Before that we didn't sell a single one. And it's not because of Gaultier. It's not because he put the idea in a public place; these ones he bought were for his private place. But him wanting them was a measure of how the chair had now become desirable. He had a nose for what is about to happen.

DIY, scaffolding, surviving

Arad

Anyway, to go back a bit, after I bought the first two chairs from the scrapyard I went to another scrapyard and bought some bus doors to be placed in the middle of the shutter. And I cut a hole in our shutter so that people could look in.

Collings

How did you know how to cut metal?

Arad

Ah, I found out.

Collings

What, when you were at the AA, or it was something you taught yourself after you left?

Arad

After I left and a bit at the AA, but frankly I wasn't so much of a manual guy.

Collings

But you still did it yourself?

Arad

Yeah, with help. I always had people around me, somehow.

Collings

Where did you get them, the people?

Arad

I don't know. From the age of eight I always had people around me. I never did anything on my own.

Collings

Well, knowing how to get help is a talent in itself.

Arad

Yeah, it's a talent.

Collings

And in the meantime no one was paying you. And you didn't really have a

job, because you were just doing your own stuff?

Arad

I didn't have a job but I started surviving on doing things for people and getting paid for it. I was there mainly at weekends, just sitting in the workshop drawing, and people would come round and they'd become paying customers. They'd tell me what it was they needed, and it'd be something like platform beds, say, and I'd do a perspective drawing of their room and work out a bed for them, there and then. I made some structures for those objects out of scaffolding. I made this cantilevered table in 1981. It was five metres long and it could swing across the space on one pivot. I remember drilling through the concrete floor, so the table could be fixed to the floor, and the hole had to be forty centimetres deep – or eighteen inches if you want inches. It was a mad, simple piece. It was sort of architectural; it was a constructed piece.

Collings

You're describing an arc in space now – what does it mean?

Arad

I'm just showing that the table pivoted at one point, and it was a simple shape with a very traditional structure of cross bracing, and it could swing in space.

Collings

Was anyone else doing scaffolding then?

Arad

Yes there was plenty of scaffolding all over the place but not as far as I knew in interiors.

Collings

It wasn't a design look, yet?

Arad

Well a scaffolding look existed, but not using actual scaffolding. It was thought of as a high-tech look, but also a kind of utilitarian look. Even though of course it was formal, not genuinely utilitarian: I mean, think of the Pompidou Centre, which went up a few years before – that went with the same look. And people were buying industrial shelves from a shop called Slingsbys. It was called Metro shelving – you know, with that zigzag mesh? Again, it wasn't a utilitarian thing, because for another thing it was probably more expensive than just using planks of wood. You see that little rusty metal thing there? There's a good example. That's a relic of the age I'm talking about.

Collings

We're sitting in your garden now and we're looking at an old rusty bit of scaffolding table thing with a concrete surface.

Arad

I mentioned how we survived in those days, well that used to be our bread and butter: scaffolding. These are called 'key clamps'. There was a

Left
Ron and Caroline Thorman in the studio/workshop in Shorts Gardens in 1982

Below
Shelving
1981

One of thousands of sketches Ron made of pieces that were custom-built from steel tubing and Kee-Klamps. 'Steel tubing, Kee-Klamps and quick drawings were the currency of the early days at One Off.'

Above and below
Platform C
Cantilevered platform bed and wardrobe
1985
Powder-coated steel tubes, Kee-Klamps,
wire-mesh panels, mirrored Venetian blinds
One Off

Platform C was one of the standardised clamps-
and-tubing designs that One Off could produce
for clients as an alternative to ordering a tailor-
made piece of furniture.

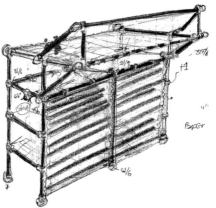

catalogue with 111 different types of joints in cast iron in eleven different sizes. This is size five and this is number ten. This is 10/5, right? I used to know them like I knew a language. The tubes can be easily cut to size. I had those materials and I had my pencil, and it was as if the structures just poured out of my pencil. People were thrilled when they came to me, describing their living room or the bedroom, and I could plot it for them there and then and throw together a scaffolding structure...

Collings

You'd make a structure for a bed?

Arad

Or shelves, or a mezzanine, or whatever.

Collings

And you were in your space in Covent Garden doing this?

Arad

Yes, and in the space there were some examples of it lying around. And I noticed that everyone came to sit down, to be drawn for, and to become a customer. It was like discovering you had some sort of power: I design in front of you and then you walk home with a very nice Oldenburgish drawing, but slightly more precise – because I used to also make a list of the measurements. The list would be something like, OK: 17×10 and 14×16, length of tube. I knew the price per metre, I had a calculator – I could give them a price there and then. I could list what kind of scaffolding fittings they needed, and what kind of tube, what kind of finish. Not only did they have the drawing but they had the price as well. And ninety per cent of them came back and paid for the bed or whatever to be made up for real. It was strange. I find it strange even now. But that was the core of my work, it financed everything else. But eventually I had to stop it – just like that, from one day to another. I said, 'No more key clamps, no more tubes, because they slow me down'. But it lasted for about six years, and it was what I lived on after I walked out of that architectural practice in Hampstead.

Public's unexpected lust for design

Collings

Once you had your studio going, and you were making things there, what did you think your job was?

Arad

I had my own freedom to play and I had my means of survival. But it was difficult for me to answer people at parties when they asked, 'What do you do?' 'Well, I'm an architect...but at the moment I...' – so I wasn't entirely free from an identity crisis. And as I said, at that time I knew nothing about the design world: the players, what they did or how it all worked. But I enjoyed it anyway. I needed a name to trade under so I called it One Off. The 'one off' notion felt correct: you know, 'I personally design everything – great!' At that time I didn't understand the pleasures of mass production, the thrill you can get from just going into production. I felt I was opposed to the commercial world: I was hands-on, individual, customized, catering for people's needs. Because it was all about these people coming into the place and me answering their needs, which they'd sit there and explain to me. And the name worked really well. And at that time I was lucky in every way: Covent Garden was fun, I had a big space there, it was the time of the high tech interest, and newspapers and magazines just started to write about this kind of thing. For example, The Face launched exactly the same time as I started One Off. And somehow I got some sort of reputation, where people knew about my place. Actually, that's also when the Architectural Association started to claim me as one of its own, and I think also it's when I started sort of 'not hiding'. I started socializing, and seeing people, and no longer hiding within that identity crisis that I had for about five minutes, when I wasn't sure what I was.

Collings

What do you mean the AA claimed you back? What did they want from you?

Arad

Oh, they wanted me to come and do things. For example, I put on an exhibition there with Nigel Coates in 1983, called 'Heads for '84'. We had people like Eduardo Paolozzi and Derek Jarman: they each had to come up with a life-size head and we put them all on a forest of pedestals. It was a sweet exhibition.

Collings

And it came just after this point where you'd been wondering who you were, what status you had?

Arad

Yeah, what am I doing? Because I thought maybe it's only temporary. I don't know what I'm doing. At the same time the Home Office was after me as well, because I was only allowed to be in the UK to go on doing my professional practice.

Collings

Of course, yes.

Arad

And slowly within that six-year period, I started employing people, people to help me to saw off the tubes, install the stuff, because I couldn't do it all myself. So these were my first designed objects besides the Rover Chair. There was this bed, this round rail bed, two curves, two poles and a mesh. Very much inspired by the Metro shelving, with that zigzag mesh. I still sleep on one. Actually everyone here in my house sleeps on beds that I first designed back then. And nowadays people email me and say, 'I have a Ron

One Off's first logo, designed by Neville Brody in 1983.

Arad bed. How much is it worth?' They want to know the value and if it's a good idea to put it in Christie's – I say no!

Collings

But the Rover Chair was different to the bed and the other things because it wasn't something made to specific requirements.

Arad

That's right, when I sold those it was more like, 'Here it is. I made this. Do you want it?' Not something I did for you, but something I did…

Collings

You just thought it up.

Arad

Yes. But that chair wasn't sold to anyone at first. It was dormant at first, just sitting in the studio. People had to see it to get the idea it was good. But that started happening through the other work, and also because the studio became a kind of club sometimes because of the parties.

Parties

Collings

What parties?

Arad

There were tons of them. The best was when one time a group of Japanese people came and said, 'Editor told us to photograph a party at One Off'. I said, 'OK, give me your phone number and I'll call you when there's a party.' 'We go home on Thursday'. I say, 'Well, look, I'm sorry…' 'Ah, we buy drinks and food.' And I say, 'No, it's impossible'. 'We pay £50 to every guest'. 'Oh, actually it's on Wednesday'. I started calling round on the phone and we put on an English tea party. There they were, asking everyone: 'Where did you buy your shoes, where did you buy your outfit, and blah blah blah – and how old are you?'

Collings

So it was a style analysis?

Arad

Yes, they wanted to copy i-D. Every picture in i-D in those days would have the caption, 'Shoes: Oxfam', that kind of thing. They had a wad of fifty-pound notes and everyone on their way out got handed one. Couples left with a hundred pounds, a lot of money in those days. And when I got the magazine I realized maybe I was sold short, because they had an amazing list of other parties they'd been to, to style-analyse, kind of global parties. I thought, 'I bet they paid the Warhol party more!'

Collings

But you felt then that you were on this global party level?

Arad

I felt I was trendy.

Left
Showroom in Neal Street, Covent Garden
1985

This picture features the shelving made from builders hods that housed books in One Off's design bookshop, a group of Rover Chairs and a screen that was designed in collaboration with glass artist Danny Lane.

Above
Heads for '84
1983

For this exhibition at One Off, which was co-curated by Nigel Coates, architects, designers and graphic designers were each commissioned to produce a life-sized head.

Below
Exhibitors at the opening event of the One Off showroom in Neal Street in 1984.

Publicity, VAT, the Home Office

Collings

What's your analysis of why you should have been trendy suddenly – you came up with some good things, but why that moment?

Arad

First of all, Covent Garden was a lucky place to find this studio. I was there at the right time and I was actually doing things, and they related to a look, the high-tech look, which was already trendy.

Collings

Yes but what do you think was the appetite that now existed that you answered? Was it design itself or was it your take on design?

Arad

People knew, because The Face kept telling them every month that matt black is in, or chrome is in. Or things like that. But there was no designing in England at all. It's difficult to imagine now but there really was very, very little.

Collings

I see – it wasn't that design existed but it was an underground thing? But how did design become trendy? Try and explain the bigger picture.

Arad

It was the boom years of the 80s. Lots of people started living by a different standard than their parents did, a different standard to where they came from. They could afford to concentrate on design. They came from a

Round Railed Bed
1981
Tubular steel, wire-mesh panels, Kee-Klamps
One Off

'The success of this bed could have put One Off in danger of becoming a furniture factory, rather than the experimental workshop it was.'

different class. Before in London the class structure slowed down that kind of thing. If you think of Germany at the time: there, people didn't want so much to associate with the past so that's why they subscribed to new architecture, new design. They wanted new symbols, a new environment. They didn't want to be constantly reminded of the terrible things of the recent past. But in London – well, I'm not a sociologist, of course. I don't want to say things are not good here, necessarily. But certainly it was obvious that people with money, the upper classes, they didn't feel they needed to buy a change of environment like the Germans did. They wanted to enforce the fashions they already knew, the environment they already knew. And actually people from the class below aspired to be like them. It was a funny kind of look they came up with to do that. I'm talking about some of my best friends now! Pop stars, real innovators in pop – the top in their field. But when it comes to using their new money to buy a new look, well, it was all sort of draped curtains, old-fashioned symbols of the old order, not really their own new symbols.

Collings

Fake aristocracy?

Arad

Yeah. So you had lots of people who found themselves for the first time with the problem – the good problem – of what to do with this new affluence. And some of it started being directed to design. And I think that came from new magazines, new colour supplements, telling people new things, showing them these new possibilities.

More stuff in boom climate

Collings

What other things were you coming up with in this climate?

Arad

Well, I took some aluminium hods for carrying bricks and I made bookshelves out of them. At that time I couldn't see a hod and not think of Muybridge and his photos of the guy carrying one – like you can't see a bicycle seat and not think of Picasso. Anyway, once I'd done the shelves I thought, 'Hmm, I'll have a book shop'. So I did a deal with the bookshop at the AA. They had a fantastic architectural bookshop there, and so at my place, through this deal, I had a design bookshop. But the books got damaged very fast.

Collings

Why, because they were all on these funny shelves?

Arad

No! The shelves work fine. It didn't work because it takes a different type of person than me to run a bookshop. But in any case the bookshop part of the studio was there at least for a while. Do you remember a giant-size multi-language style and art magazine called The Manipulator? It started then and the bookshop was an official point of sale for it. So there was that. But also we put on exhibitions for other creative people. We displayed the work of designers like Tom Dixon and Danny Lane. And Katsuhiko Hibino – he's an artist. And Willy Moser, the photographer from The Manipulator. Actually Hibino, this artist, was a household name then in Japan. It turned out he had a chat show on Japanese TV. But I didn't know that when we showed him. He just walked in one day and we became friends. Anyway, they were all different types of creative people from different fields. I remember being so frustrated phoning Time Out – Time Out was in Covent Garden then – and the exhibitions editor refused to step outside to look at these shows, because she couldn't understand what they were all supposed to be – there wasn't a clear category for them.

Collings

But there was an appetite for it. Something had happened in society that meant there was an opening for this stuff, this extra stuff.

Arad

Yes. I invented my profession. I didn't know what it was. I mean, even on the business side it was confusing. When I started there was a big VAT strike, and I'd been selling and I had no idea I had to keep records. I thought you paid for something and that was it. I didn't know you had to tell somebody about it. I didn't know how to keep invoices. I just threw all receipts away, of course. And then when the strike was over they came to me.

Right
A New Descending Staircase
1985
Reclaimed railway sleepers, concrete, electronics

In this cantilevered staircase, which was installed in the studio/showroom in Neal Street, each step was a 'key': a trigger for a powerful synthesizer. As a person walked up or down the staircase, their movements produced a randomly-generated musical sequence.

Below
The Shorts Garden studio sign resting on a swivelling six-metre cantilevered table.

Cone
Chair and table
1986
Welded mild steel, aluminium, slate, glass
and rubber
One Off

Ron and Caroline Thorman sitting on Cone
pieces in 1987. 'This range emerged in order
for us to practice our welding techniques!'

Collings

With the VAT bill?

Arad

Exactly, it was really bad. I interviewed people for someone to come and
help me get out of it, and that's how I met Caroline Thorman. She became
my partner and still works with me today. But anyway, slowly, slowly, this
Covent Garden studio had became a business. I had the façade, I painted it
silver, and I had these big letters: ONE OFF. But it was all under the cloud
of me being always on the verge of being deported. At one point, I was
given 24 days to leave. The head of the Design Council at that time, Lord
Riley, wrote a letter to the then Home Secretary, David Waddington, saying,
'I've seen a letter signed by you, but I don't believe you've written it,
because this letter was written by an idiot'. Amazing isn't it? It's a good
lesson in letter writing. And, 'What are you doing, deporting him – Ron
Arad is an asset!' I didn't really know what it was I did then that made him
feel he had to support me.

Collings

As you say, there wasn't an already established market for what you were
doing and not even a name for it?

Arad

No but there was all this publicity in colour supplements and, you know,
The Face running articles that would say things like, 'Most influential
names of the 80s – Ron Arad, designer' kind of thing. People used to say,
'You're very good at PR'. 'I'm not doing any PR at all – what do you want
from me?' What I thought I was doing wasn't the same as the image of me
that was building up, this 'designer'. I'd show them a rocking chair I'd
done, in about 1983, I think, and I'd say, 'This is my first piece of really
what you could call design. 'It represents the first point where I knew that
what I was doing was design. The first thing I did that wasn't a kind of one-
liner based on the concept of the ready-made.

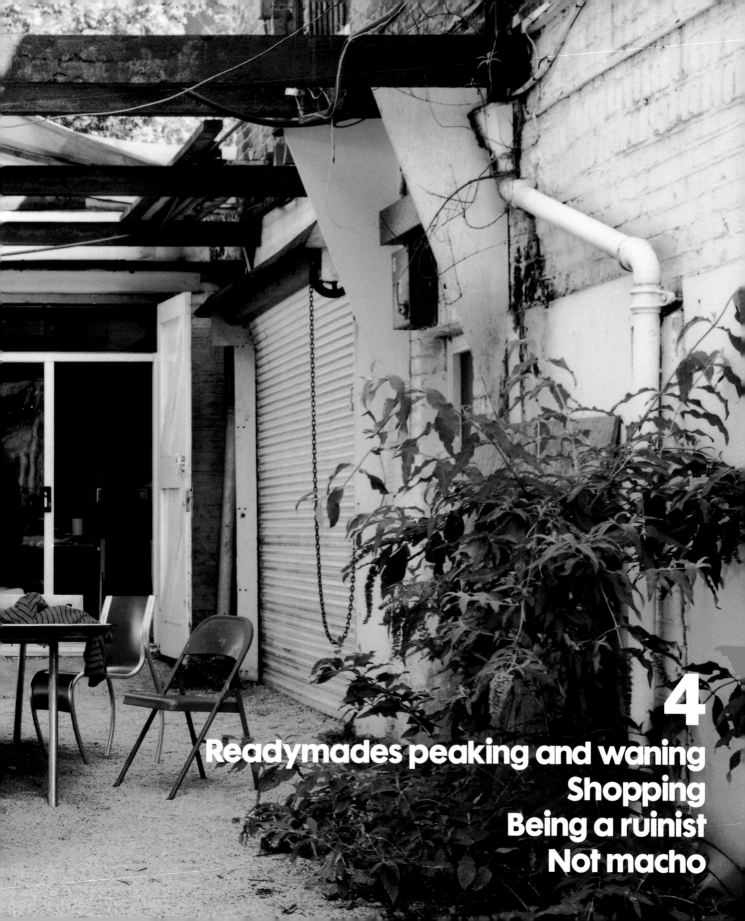

4
Readymades peaking and waning
Shopping
Being a ruinist
Not macho

Readymades peaking and waning

Collings

So you made this rocking chair in 83 and this was your first bit of design where you weren't drawing on ideas from art about readymades – where you designed something for yourself, from scratch?

Arad

It was called the Rocking Chair, it had to be called that to tell people that it rocks, because it didn't actually have rockers; it had a movement like a scissor. So again it wasn't a readymade, it was something I designed from scratch. It wasn't stylish, it wasn't designed for style, it was designed to carry a mechanical idea. If you have, like, an unchained parallelogram – or scissors is another way of describing it – you can get a new kind of movement. The important thing was the mechanical idea and therefore when I had to design it I designed a tube that was very near to the clamps and tools that I was using before, but instead of the cast iron fittings, it was bent in a radius. Not surprisingly, very similar to the loops and radii of Modern Movement furniture. I didn't think I was inventing a style there. I just left it in the style of 'modern furniture' – I say modern, I mean modern-period furniture.

Collings

What principle do you think is in there?

Arad

The principle is that everything should be based on something that didn't exist before. In this case it wasn't the idiom, the Modern Movement idiom was taken almost as given, but concealed within it was the newness of the mechanism of the movement. And I think that that perverse desire, that

Concrete Stereo
1983
Concrete, hi-fi components, silicon
Edition of approximately 10
One Off

'This piece evolved from a merged interest and activity in both electronics and concrete. Very, very few of the stereos were made. They occasionally appear at auction – we want to buy one back because we don't have one, but we're always beaten by a higher bidder.'

everything I do should contain something that is new (to me anyway), or that design is about something that wasn't there before you designed it – I think if I look back I see that what we did was an act of design rather than assembly. The Rocking Chair was the object I came up with after I decided I had to stop doing readymades. I didn't know I was going to be a designer. I became one through doing about six readymade pieces that got a lot of attention and publicity, where I was described as a designer.

Collings

Tell me about some of those readymades.

Arad

One of them was a concrete stereo: a hi-fi encased in concrete. It was thought to be pretty subversive and interesting. There was a concrete amp and a concrete turntable. I like it now as an object of beauty: the knobs and sockets and resistors, and the pebbles and sand, all mixed together. What I did was, I assembled the amplifier, say, without a chassis. And we'd then hang it on the washing line and spray some special material, like tar, to make it waterproof. And we sprayed the deck separately. I lowered them into setting concrete and as it was setting I could actually arrange the thing casually, as if it wasn't arranged. There was a lot of technique involved. I used to have to chip it a bit with the chisel. I thought, 'Hm, with Bang & Olufsen you can't produce something and then chip it – and it's better!' And there was another good one: a remote control light. It was based on the automatic car aerial. I remember driving to work one day and I saw a Jag in front of me. And all of a sudden I saw the aerial having an erection. You know, when you switch the radio on in those expensive cars…? I remember researching and finding Nippon Antenna, a Japanese company. I started looking into motors and things, and I had an electronic boffin from the Black Country constructing these things for me. And this light could turn 360 degrees, contract down to zero and extend to one metre.

Collings

When you say a light, it was a beam of light or…?

Arad

No, no…a halogen light bulb with a cable attached. It looked like a fishing rod, a remote-control fishing rod. And it was really a readymade. Remember televisions used to have remote controls connected to a cable? I used that. And somehow for some people this light was irresistible. It's all silly, right? There's nothing easier than leaning over towards your anglepoise and directing the light with your hand. But the feeling of power you have if you can do it from here, without moving: there's the light and then zip! It moves! And these things now fetch colossal prices at Sotheby's and Christie's. I have one myself, still. We weren't very good at keeping stuff then, we couldn't afford to. So that lamp was another readymade, but a very sophisticated readymade. It was like an 'assisted readymade', really.

And before that there were the scaffolding things, and before them the Rover Chairs.

Collings

Do you think all these things were primarily visual, their nature was visual and their appeal was visual?

Arad

I don't think it's purely visual. I think first of all, it had some wit and some humour. It never took itself very solemnly. It was just 'This is what I do'.

Shopping

Collings

So you had had a series of triumphs really, of what were basically readymades, and they made you into a designer?

Arad

Yes – I didn't have a single error in the readymade area! And if you go to 1980s newspapers and magazines now, there are tons of pages of that stuff. And then people like Joseph, in fashion, gets excited. 'Shall we do an exhibition in Sloane Street?' – 'Yeah, sure'. And whatever Joseph shows in Sloane Street...

Collings

Everyone else in the high street would do, too?

Arad

No, there's about a hundred shops in the world, in New York...

Collings

Oh, so not on the high street?

Arad

No, on Melrose Avenue, in LA, that kind of level.

Collings

Once it's in Joseph these other top places are all on to it?

Arad

Yes. If he were to have a white donkey in his window, there was guaranteed to be eighty shops in the world with the same thing. I don't know what happens now but that's how it was then. There was a shop called Maxfield Blue on Melrose Avenue. It was the only one with a car park, a significant feature in LA. And one space was reserved for Lois Battram. She comes once a year to the shop and she spends a lot, in fact she buys the shop. She lives somewhere and for some reason I'm there and so I meet her. Then I'm in the shop and the owner's there, a guy called Tommy. And I told him, 'I met some friends of yours last night.' He said, 'Friends? I don't have friends. Friends want discount'. Anyway I talked to him because he began to buy from us after we sold stuff at Joseph. And now he had to have all the stuff. He had to have Rover Chairs, Aerial Lights and later the Concrete Stereo. And there I also saw Issey Miyake buying an Aerial Lamp. Tommy

Aerial Light
1981
Car aerial, spun aluminium, die-cast aluminium, electrical components, halogen bulb
One Off

A sketch drawn the year the light was designed.

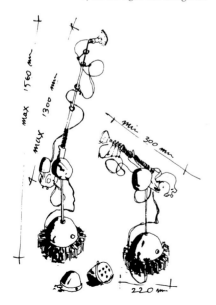

wouldn't bother introducing me. We are great friends now – Miyake is fantastic – but back then he was more like a distant hero.

Being a ruinist

Collings

Once you affectionally dubbed Jean Paul Gaultier a punk copyist, I thought you were a bit the same yourself, weren't you – with your DIY aesthetic?

Arad

Well, in a way, although when that's said of me I always have to think they got the wrong guy, because I'm really not a punk type. But the epitome of

Right
Aerial Light
1981
Car aerial, spun aluminium, die-cast aluminium, electrical components, halogen bulb
One Off

'This piece demonstrates the early wonders of remote control. Because it came out around the same time as the film, this light earned me (on the cover of Blueprint) the title "Mad Max".'

Below
Aerial Light
Infra-red remote control unit
1981

The direction pads are marked with Ron's fingerprints, the handwriting is taken from a Letraset transfer and the 'patent pending' is a statement lifted from the text on the bottom of the Letraset sheet. 'The light's remote control unit extended the ad-hoc readymadeness of the light itself.'

Interior of Bazaar/John Paul Gaultier for Men
1983
London

Above: a preliminary sketch for the design of a
shop in South Molton Street. Below: 'We made
the Pompeian figures by first making an imprint
of people in a mouldable plastic mattress (our
Transformer Mattresses), and then setting
concrete into the cavity. The concrete wall was
made by casting it on the floor on-site, then
raising it in sections to clad the existing wall.'

that kind of thing was the Concrete Stereo, of course. That, and then later on a project I wound up doing for the Gaultier shop, got me the title of 'Ruinist' in France: Ron Arad, Ruinist. And then here in Britain they had labels like Post-Holocaust and Mad Max. And over there, in Paris, as well as Ruinist they also had the idea of the Destroyed Look. In 1986 they celebrated the tenth anniversary of the Pompidou Centre, and they had an exhibition for it, 'Les Nouvelle Tendances', for which they invited all the influential people in the design world, the active ones. This was a list of big people and I was on it, the youngest one. The reason they invited me is because they thought it would be good to have someone who's a Ruinist or a Destroy guy. And so that exhibition for the tenth anniversary of the Pompidou was another turning point for me – and like the previous turning points it came completely out of the blue.

Collings

Looking back now, with hindsight, what do you think explains this high culture success?

Arad

I think now what I thought at the time, that whatever it was they wanted me to be, wasn't really what I thought I was. It's hard to explain their side, I can only give my own side. I used to deny that I'm rebelling against anything. I said, 'This is not destruction, this is not being destructive, this is pointing at beauty where it's normally hidden. It's a positive thing. Nothing to do with Beirut, say, and nothing to do with war – nothing to do with anything'. I used to say, 'I guess, if that's what you see in it, ruination, destruction, and so on, who am I to argue? If this stereo reminds you of broken buildings, I can't help it. But that's not the intention'. The theme of the exhibition at the Pompidou centre was The Habitation of the Future. But in the end everyone does what he does – Mendini does Mendini's stuff and Hans Hollein does his. Everyone pedals his merchandise. We had a week, all the exhibitors together, and there was Starck there – young Philippe Starck.

Collings

Was he your immediate rival, the one most like you?

Arad

No, he was a lot more successful. Also, being successful in Paris means something different than being successful in London.

Collings

I asked because I wondered if you still thought you were alone on your wave of success? Or did you now feel you were fighting with competitors and peers, and with people who wanted to copy you and rip you off?

Arad

Neither of those precisely. I was happy to be successful and happy to be in that exhibition with other people who did something like what I did. I did make a soulmate there: this Spanish guy from Barcelona, Mariscal. He was

Sticks and Stones
Baling machine for chairs
1986

'We made this installation piece for 'Les
Nouvelles Tendances', an exhibition held at the
Centre Georges Pompidou in Paris in 1986.
Parisians were invited to bring chairs to the
museum, place them on a conveyor belt and
watch them be turned into bricks. Over the six
months the exhibition lasted, an ever-growing
wall of compacted chairs was constructed. After
the exhibition closed, the machine spent a
number of years travelling to several locations
world-wide.''

the next-youngest person after me and we both sneered a little at the others.
I mean Starck was beginning to be an event in Paris: the first design star.
At least the first to come from France after a long time.

Collings

Yes, he did toothbrushes or something, didn't he?

Arad

A bit later, but yes.

Collings

They were bendy?

Arad

Very French, very stylized toothbrushes. He's a very witty stylist. But, yes,
I felt good, but also I was a misfit there.

Collings

Why?

Arad

Well, because of the programme. 'Habitation for the Future'. In my
statements to the organizers I said I wasn't interested in the future. All
I could do was make it come a little faster. And the only way I could do that
was by destroying some of the – well, maybe sort of living up to the false
pretext on which I was invited, this idea of the Ruinist. I said the most
important machine in the car industry is really the machine that destroys
cars, because it makes room for new ones. And when you move into a new
place, you don't open the wardrobe and say, 'Let's see what I have to wear
here'. Your clothes are your own. You bought them for yourself alone. But
with design and furniture, and things like that, people don't expect changes
to come so fast. There are still the same standards, the same heights all the
time. So my project for that exhibition was that I built a huge machine in
the Pompidou Centre that started with a conveyor belt. And I invited
Parisians to come to the museum with their favourite piece of furniture –
or their least favourite piece – and to place it on the conveyor belt. And then
it was crunched and compressed. I said if they wanted the future to come
they had to make a sacrifice.

Collings

You did Michael Landy fifteen years before him?

Arad

Yes, I talked to him about it the other day. But mine was a little different.
In fact it was more like César. And to show Parisians I knew a little history,
I called it Cesarian Operation.

Collings

You wanted to refer to the squashed car guy: the artist, César, from the
1960s? It's remarkable that we don't really have an equivalent of the
Pompidou here: there isn't that excitement about art and design and
architecture, and arguments, and attitudes, and so on, all being
theatricalized in that way or given a big public form…

Arad

Yes, this machine was an amazing thing. And it was pretty incredible to see people trying to protect chairs from going on the conveyor belt: 'Oh no! Ne peut pas faire ça!'

Collings

Someone would agree to put his chair up on the belt and then someone else would be horrified?

Arad

Yes – you know, the fifteen seconds of fame for a chair that no one looked at before? The machine ran for six months. Then I got a letter from the Pompidou centre saying they'd sold it to Louis Vuitton for performances where they got rid of counterfeit Vuitton bags.

Collings

Ha ha – what a mad world! It's like Zoolander.

Arad

Yeah but that wasn't the end of it. I said, 'Hang on a second, the machine is mine as well. It is not only yours'– because I got sponsorship for it from people in England. So the Pompidou people needed my signature to go ahead with the sale. And I was in Milan, in an exhibition there, and the Pompidou people came and said, 'Well, if you don't sign you have to collect it within three days' – six tons of machinery. So then the owner of Vitra – do you know them?

Collings

No, what is it?

Arad

One of the most progressive furniture manufacturers, it's Swiss. They were the first people to employ Frank Gehry to build outside America, and he built the Vitra Design Museum in Weil am Rhein. The owner of Vitra, who I didn't know at all well, put his hand on my shoulder and said, 'Don't worry, Ron. If you want, I can send a truck to collect it from the Pompidou Centre tomorrow'. And I said, 'Yeah, OK'.

Collings

So now Vitra had given you an exhibition, too?

Arad

Yeah. It was the crushing machine and the rest of the studio collection – the first exhibition in this new Gehry museum.

Collings

And what was the machine crunching up?

Arad

All sorts of things: chairs, stuff like that.

Collings

And Swiss people brought their chairs to be crunched up?

Arad

Yes but it's in the middle of nowhere, so not so many people. And then

Sticks and Stones
Preparatory sketch for the installation at the Centre Georges Pompidou in Paris
1986

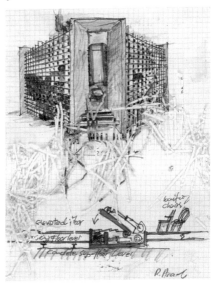

about three years ago the Pompidou Centre bought it back from Vitra, for the permanent collection.

Not macho

Collings

Do you ever think of your early work as macho? You know: that beaten steel look? The concrete stuff, the scaffolding?

Arad

A hammer used to be one of my main tools – a rubber hammer.

Collings

To beat-up the thing, yeah...

Arad

I'd take a piece of steel and beat it until it admits it's comfortable, kind of. Other people might look at that and see a meaning there, but it was never a macho act for me – I mean, I can't help it: I was big and strong and I could do things. At the same time I do things that are very delicate and light.

Collings

You never thought of it as an issue? No one ever mentioned it before?

Arad

Well, they did. There's a really nice introduction to a book we did on this place, One Off Three, which Ettore Sottsass wrote for us. He described the first time he saw things that I did. He said, 'Is there a new type of people now that are stronger than us?' I mean, it was, 'Who are these new people, what is it they do?' He said he was threatened by it. And then he learned how Peter Cook described it as like a big dog that you are scared of initially, and it takes you a while to see that actually it's a friendly, cuddly dog. But my main welder in the old days was a girl, Rachel Reynolds. In Covent Garden, Paul Smith used to be very taken by her looks – he only did menswear in those days. But he said, 'You know, I am very inspired by your Rachel'. She was a girl by night and a boy by day. So maybe the mistake is attributing strength, and that kind of thing, to males only.

Collings

Oh quite! But on the whole do you think the design world and the architecture world is a bit masculine?

Arad

We can't fail to notice that. There's really only one woman architect...

Collings

Right – the star...

Arad

...to every hundred men.

Collings

Oh I thought you meant there really was only one, and you were going to tell me who she was! In fact I really can only think of one.

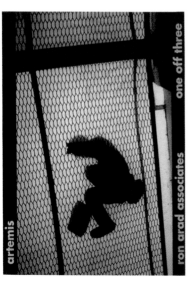

The cover of One Off Three, a book published by Artemis in 1991 that documented the design and construction of a new studio space for Ron Arad Associates in Chalk Farm, London.

Chair By Its Cover
1989
Stainless steel, mild steel, wooden chair
Edition of 20
One Off

'This piece was a reflection on the whole activity of readymades, the design of new pieces and design's unessentialness. The first two pieces in this series were inscribed on their backs with back-to-front writing that read, on the first, "Why bark if you can have a dog?", and, on the second, "Why have a dog if you can bark yourself?".'

Arad

Zaha Hadid?

Collings

Yeah, and I know her name only because she made the Turner Prize speech one year, and also because you mentioned her earlier in your stories about the AA.

Arad

There's her, there's a few others, and there used to be Eileen Gray, Linda Bo Bardi and Gae Aulenti.

Collings

That used to be the case in the art world a lot, too. I mean, it's relatively recent that there's been a huge explosion of women stars in the art world.

Arad

Yeah and also there was a genre called Women's Art...

Collings

That's right. And it's only recently been got rid of, so it's taken for granted that a woman would be an artist and she needn't necessarily be doing Women's Art.

Arad

When we interviewed people for the design course at the Royal College – I mean it's a little better now, but hardly any women applied. It's really not enough for a healthy social group. But you know, if you go back to the definition I suggested earlier, of design being a matter of imposing your will on materials to perform a function – well, some people would classify imposing your will on anything at all as pretty macho. But I leave it to Germaine Greer to work that out.

Collings

OK, let's leave it to her then.

5
Doors strangely closed
Bricks, Neo-Geo,
lights going on and off
Being serious

Doors strangely closed

Collings

Here you were in the 1980s having all these art gallery shows, but operating still somehow in a parallel universe as far as art is concerned; art's still got its doors closed to you, really. It might open them to run out and have a bit of a fight and then go back again, but that's all.

Arad

That's right.

Collings

The Saatchi gallery was up and running by now, wasn't it – it opened in 1985.

Arad

I'll tell you what occurred with Saatchi: they asked us for a concrete stereo for a commercial. And we would've given one to them but we didn't have any. And then I see a commercial on TV and there it is! They made one out of styrofoam. So we spent some money on a lawyer and I get such a filthy letter from their lawyer, saying that if we pursue this they will sue us for libel, little us, big them – and we didn't call their bluff! So now we're not having this conversation!

Collings

That was the end of your chances for a show with Saatchi?

Arad

I don't suppose he personally even knew about it. It was other people. And also they got me when I was young. Today I wouldn't let them get away with it.

Collings

You said that even though you'd started designing things for real and accepting that you weren't doing a kind of variation on a Duchamp idea of

Cartier Tables
Early sketch for the installation at the
Fondation Cartier, Paris
1994

readymades, nevertheless you still didn't think of yourself as a designer. And from what you've said one can see you coming out of art, and now often you seem to be taken seriously in an art context. And yet as we've said already, actually the doors are still closed.

Arad

But when you say that, it assumes someone's knocking! And I can't help thinking when I see art – successful art – how thin it is sometimes. But one doesn't get neurotic about it. OK, it's thin but it's only another sentence in an ongoing conversation. I mean, let's not panic. And you can go to homes of people who'd have Gerhard Richter on the walls, and so on, and you look at the carpet – at the tables, the sofas, the chairs – and it's laughable. You see the way their taste operates and the way it's only propped up by fake class. And there'll be a Bill Woodrow mop-and-bucket sculpture on the carpet, that every new cleaner tries to tidy away. Personally I'd take the carpet away first! But you know – one doesn't expect everything to make sense.

Bricks, Neo-Geo, lights going on and off

Collings

We've mentioned Haim Steinbach and Jeff Koons in the 1980s a couple of times – did you like those artists or despise them?

Arad

I liked the things that came out of the first Neo Geo wave – Koons's flower puppy and his shiny rabbit were both fantastic, but I don't care about the rest.

Collings

Did you think that Neo-Geo in the 1980s had anything to do with you in its take on modern design? Or did you think that wasn't exactly what the interest was? Its interest was more a philosophical comment on design? And you were really doing design, or what? I mean, given your ambivalence about what it was you really thought you were doing then?

Arad

No, it's what you just said: I still think I was actually doing things while those artists were doing things about things; about things that we – people in my profession, of making things – do. I used to say, 'You know, we make the cars. Someone else cuts them in half and puts them in a gallery'.

Collings

What about the art that's trendy now?

Arad

I don't mind it. Martin Creed, his lights going on and off – I was very happy he won the Turner Prize, because it's no skin off my nose. It's nice when you think, 'How can anyone be more minimal than Carl Andre's bricks?'

Jeff Koons
Rabbit
1986

And I don't mind seeing everyone upset. I also don't mind art being written about in the front pages of all the tabloids, even if it's hate.

Being serious

Cartier Tables

1994
Fondation Cartier, Paris

The installation for the inaugural exhibition at the Fondation Cartier was made up of 40 super-reflective tables arranged in a paving formation. 'At first glance, the viewer found it difficult to tell the difference between the negative and the positive. In reflecting the movement of cars, trees and the changing light, the installation enjoyed the unprotected space of the totally transparent gallery.'

Collings

What other details or nuances of difference are there between your own attitudes and those of artists?

Arad

Well, I don't know – you know, I was recently asked to put on an installation for the opening exhibition of the Cartier Foundation. When they moved to Boulevard Raspail – do you know the building by Jean Nouvel? It's in Paris? Anyway, for the opening exhibition they had Richard

Artschwager on one side and me on the other. And in the Pompidou Centre, at the same time, there was an exhibition of Ettore Sottsass. And there is a tremendous similarity between Ettore Sottsass and Artschwager: they both do exaggerated patterns, they do Formica wood patterns, sort of flirting with bad taste. And they both draw identically: the same sort of line drawing with a bit of colour. And I said to Artschwager, 'You know there is an exhibition of Sottsass on here'. And he said, 'Who?' They're exactly the same age, both born in 1917, but he had no idea who Sottsass was. 'Have you heard of Memphis?' 'No'. 'Ah'. In the morning (we stayed in the same hotel) his partner says, 'That Italian you told us we should go and see, what's his name?' And you know they went to see him. But in a funny way both me and Artschwager were showing furniture: he was showing object things, jokey furniture, and I did, like, a full-blown installation, but the basic unit of it was a piece of furniture: a dining table. Jean Nouvel, who I mentioned, talked about virtuality and transparency, and about something that I personally like very much – the space not having the cold perfection of an art gallery. You know – as opposed to the Saatchi Gallery where, if you place a thing in the middle of that space, well, everything, even that shark, will acquire a meaning.

Collings

Yes, that's right. Everything seems significant because of the swankiness of the building.

Arad

Because of the aura of the gallery, right. But in this new Cartier Foundation building, the art is really on its own – there's no support from the architecture. The sky's outside and it's a glass wall, so the outside space is right there on the inside, felt to be totally right there inside the building. There're trees outside, the sun shines, the weather changes…

Collings

I see, and you were showing these shiny metal tables that caught all the reflections?

Arad

Forty of them, yes, and when they were new they were absolutely like mirrors. They reflected the outside and you could see every change of the light. And also they take a bit of reality outside and frame it. It's an art gallery but instead of the art being on the walls, in paintings by Monet, it is…

Collings

Just molten-blob shiny metal shapes?

Arad

Yes, you looked at it, and you couldn't tell which is real, which is a reflection, which is positive, which is negative. The installation changed with the different light throughout the day, and it was different without people and different with them. And it's all about pictures in a gallery.

Cartier Table

1994
Laser-cut mirror-polished stainless-steel, raw-steel
Edition of 40
Ron Arad Studio

'After the exhibition closed, each of the tables ended up in a different part of the world.'

Collings

Are you saying there's a philosophical difference between what you were doing and what Artschwager was doing? Or philosophically they are the same but nobody will admit that – because it levels-out something that people believe should be hierarchical, with art on top?

Arad

What I think is that this was the opening exhibition in a piece of architecture. And I did an installation. The component was, instead of like Sarah Lucas going and finding a readymade table, the component was actually a table. I designed it. At the end of the exhibition all the tables were sold and dispersed around the world.

Collings

It had a meaning side, a practical side, a social side, it acknowledged its setting and it acknowledged the literal transparency of the gallery.

Arad

Yes. For me it was an easy exhibition, because I just did the drawing of one thing. And I had a lot of students from Paris helping to set up the 'paving' pattern. And it was just as I'd imagined it. I arrived three days before the opening to install, but I was finished in half a day.

Collings

So this whole Cartier Foundation exhibition had ironic furniture done by an artist – Artschwager – and then ironic furniture done by a designer – you.

Arad

Actually the garden outside, or what would seem to be something like a garden, was another artwork. It was by Lothar Baumgarten.

Collings

The conceptual artist from the 1970s?

Arad

Yes. He wouldn't allow me to continue the table formation past the glass exterior of the building, which is something I wanted to do. He said, 'I want to keep my garden clean'. It became like a poem. We used to recite it – the people from my studio, and me – 'I want to keep my garden clean'.

Collings

The conceptual artist is all about purity and you're about impurity?

Arad

Everyone is typecast. You can't complain about being typecast.

Collings

No, but what do you think about these two stereotypes of pure and impure? I mean, in your case. Your objects seem to me to be all about...

Arad

About purity?

Collings

No, I think your objects really are deliberately impure. They make a statement about something, on top of being simply visually nice: for

Cartier Tables
1994
Fondation Cartier, Paris

Visitors to the Fondation Cartier installation exploring the reflective potential of the Cartier tables.

example, they say, 'This is modern individuality: I am drawing freehand!'
Arad

OK, I'll buy impurity. What I am saying is that if it's really that, I'm very fanatic about achieving it, very fussy.
Collings

The showdown between you and Baumgarten is because he's concerned to be seen as serious, and that means he's got to construct everyone else around him – in this case, you – as not so serious.
Arad

I don't even think it was derogatory. I don't think it was about me. I think it was about this garden. But how can I say it? It wasn't cheerful. It wasn't pleasant. And there are other ways of going about that kind of thing. And also the garden was to mature in about five years – yet this was the opening event. You had to take his word for it that there was going to be a garden there!

6
Interesting views on chairs
Crude to refined
More angles on chairs
Welding, polishing and the decorative
More decorative

New Orleans
Armchair
1999
Pigmented polyester reinforced with fibreglass
Edition of 18 unique pieces
Handmade by Ron for The Gallery Mourmans

Interesting views on chairs

Collings

Tell me about your painted chairs. There are lots of nice 'off' things about them: off colours, off materials. To me they seem very free, like paintings – a lot of transparency, layering, open marks – but all handled in this rather finessed way.

Arad

Many artists and painters make a point of not liking them. For me they were a kind of holiday from...well, subject matter. I don't have to think about it: I mean, I don't have to think about, you know, what shapes to paint, because the shape of the chair is already given. So I can do the painting without worrying about bad art. I'm not inhibited by that debate.

Collings

You don't have to think of something clever to ironize your brushstroke, or justify what it is you're doing?

Arad

Yeah, I don't have to hide my skills and I don't have to flog my skills. I can just go ahead and do it. And every time I was about to paint one I'd have a plan of what I was going to do, and in the end it was never remotely like that.

Collings

So it really is like being a painter.

Arad

I think so! And also it's very difficult. You have to stop yourself from dripping. You don't want the piece to be too Pollocky. It's very difficult for me not to Pollock, because that stuff I use drips like honey, and it's very seductive.

Right
New Orleans
Armchair
1999
Pigmented polyester reinforced with fibreglass
Edition of 18 unique pieces
Handmade by Ron for The Gallery Mourmans

Ron painting polyester into the mould of a
New Orleans chair.

Collings

Is the chair material that you're painting on always transparent? A mark made with a transparent material on something that's also transparent will tend to look rather lovely anyway...

Arad

No, what I'm painting on isn't transparent, but it is like drawing on glass. It's not like painting on a chair, but building the coloured layers from the outside in. I start painting it inside the mould, layer by layer, in varying degrees of transparency, covering the previous layer in the process. It's only when you eventually remove the mould that you can see through the layers that were trapped in that mould. Only then can you see what you've got.

Collings

How many did you do – why didn't you go on forever?

Arad

I did twenty-five of the first series and then eighteen of a bigger one. The first series was the Pic Chairs, a cheap pun on chairs and pictures, and the other series is the New Orleans. New Orleans because the 'Big Easy' is the nickname of the city of New Orleans and the Big Easy Chair expired as a limited edition, so I came up with New Orleans. This was making chairs in a mould with coloured substance that made the surface look like a painting. But it was actually...the paint was the raw material to make the chair.

Collings

Did you do one a day, or ten, or what?

Arad

Every Friday I did one. Sometimes, when the deadline was approaching, I did maybe two, even three. Just me and an assistant.

Collings

And was it genuinely as fun to do as it looks?

Arad

Oh yeah.

Collings

So you experienced fun?

Arad

Yeah.

Collings

And you were satisfied and thought, 'That's good'?

Arad

Yeah, and they all sold out on the first showing.

Collings

Wow! And they only took a day?

Arad

No, the whole process takes longer. They're made of polyester. The mould is made of fibreglass. It's made in four smooth parts for reflective smooth surfaces. You can see here, with this one that we're looking at on the

computer screen now, how that tartan was the first layering of what was to become tartanish.

Collings

Yes, there's layering – I can see that.

Arad

Here, if you look on the computer screen at this sequence of images of me doing one of them, you can see I first painted the white but then I left the edges and then I painted the black. It made a certain type of mark and I wanted to try that again. It worked so well, and also someone wanted one just the same. But I found I couldn't repeat, it always failed. And then with this other one, you can see there's some Pollocking and there's all the tricks: palette knife and trowels, and so on. But actually the transparency is a lot richer than Pollock, I think. In fact the Pollock show was on here at the Tate Gallery when I did them, and I was impressed by how dull it was – not as an event, of course. But the canvases, I wanted to love them more than I did. He is great but I wanted them to be more potent as pieces of colour or texture, and they weren't. I mean, the photographs now seem more important to me than that show. The ones where you see him working on the paintings on the floor. You can see they're not wild paintings at all. Anyway, when I finish these chair paintings we paint the last layer white.

Collings

What do you mean – inside it's white?

Arad

Yes, it gives light to the whole thing.

Collings

So where Impressionist paintings are typically on a white ground, so the colour really glows, in your case it's like putting the white underneath an Impressionist painting as the last stage instead of the first?

Arad

Yes. And each one had a number. This one we're looking at was number three.

Collings

Is it always painted into them like that?

Arad

Yes, and I wrote things on the back of them.

Collings

Little messages?

Arad

It was random stuff.

Collings

Did you ever turn out a painted chair that you sold but you really thought it was a dud?

Arad

No, not really – except one that I thought was really ugly.

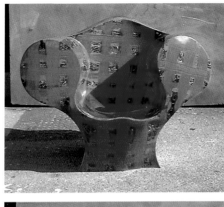

New Orleans

Armchairs

1999

Pigmented polyester reinforced with fibreglass

Edition of 18 unique pieces

Handmade by Ron for The Gallery Mourmans

'Usually when you take a New Orleans out of
the mould, it's better than you bargained for –
although we did dislike one of them immensely
(this one, however, loved by its owner).'

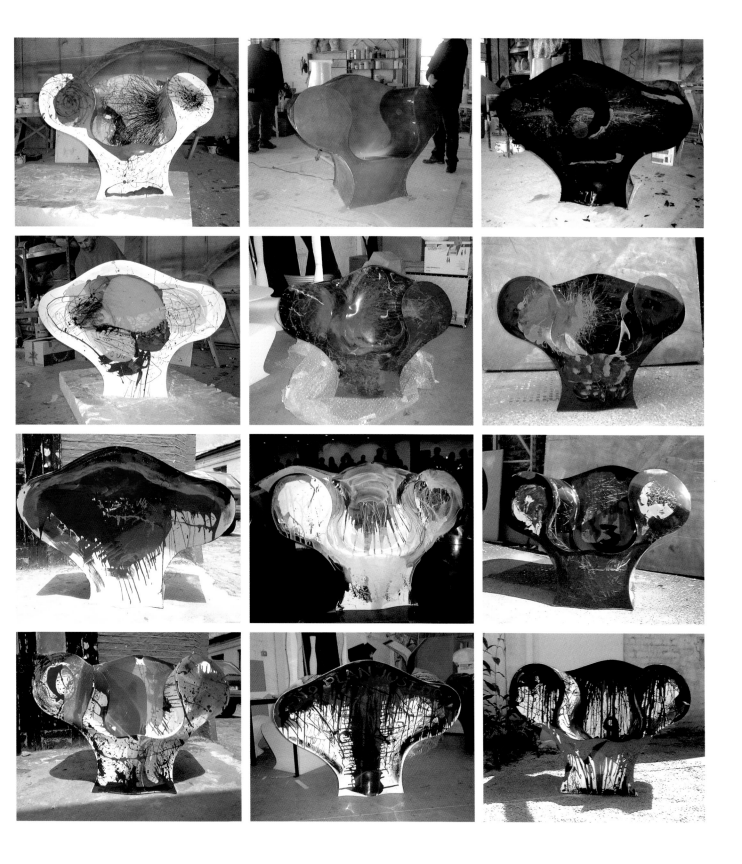

Crude to refined

Collings

What do you think is the difference between your painted chairs and the chairs and sofas, and so on, of the Viennese artist, Franz West – the way he paints those objects of his?

Arad

I think when I'm doing it, the chair in itself is paramount. It's more considered as a piece of furniture. I mean, this chair evolved.

Collings

So when you say the difference with Franz West is that your chair is more considered as a chair...

Arad

I mean it has a life as a shape. It's more of a chair.

Collings

But you both use a similar language of painting: flowing, weightless, gestural abstraction. He sometimes uses patterned fabrics but he paints a lot, as well.

Arad

Well, this language is weightless because I changed the gravity all the time. Sometimes I would turn the chair over and it would pour upwards. Which is so much fun. I mean, some painters – Ian Davenport, say – can just do that as painting, but here there's an alibi for it: which is a chair. And I wouldn't have them any other way now.

Collings

This drippy one that we are looking at now, it's just black and white. There's no meaning. But no one knows what the meaning of a Franz West is either. On the other hand everyone knows that you're doing fun abstract painting in the context of a chair, and no other level of significance is required, really. But with Franz West we just don't know. He's this humorous, amusing, joint-smoking old shabby guy. We don't know if his work is heavy or light, silly or serious. The only information other than the evidence of your own eyes, which for me is very positive, is all this anaemic strangulated fake intellectual hot air about him in the press releases, and so on, or in articles about him in art magazines, where you're being asked to pretend it's all got something to do with Hegel. And I always think if you go down that road you're kind of doomed, really.

Arad

One thing I know that definitely isn't hot air is that these chairs were our company's bread and butter – you know, this is an expensive operation here.

Collings

Yes, it points up an interesting bit of hypocrisy about the art world. The art world has mystery, the design world has function; but the art world's

Franz West
Docustühle (Docu chairs)
1997

This installation was set up in the artist's studio in Vienna.

mystery often isn't all that mysterious any more. No one believes it's particularly profound with Franz West. They accept the unconvincing stuff they read about him, because that's a routine that goes with the territory. On the other hand, they know that routine doesn't exist with design: there simply isn't that mystery context there. So one's a mystery that no one believes in, and one's a non-mystery because no one asks for a mystery in the first place.

Arad

For some people there would be mystery here.

Collings

There would?

Arad

Yeah, because this is the ugly one, I think.

Collings

It looks great!

Arad

I know the owner is very, very happy with it. The person that got it is very happy, but to me...

Collings

I'm getting a bit suspicious of myself now, because I haven't seen one yet that I didn't think looked great.

Arad

Well, that one is not good, I'm telling you.

More angles on chairs

Collings

When we were talking earlier we batted back and forth a bit about what the differences and similarities might be between your painted chairs and the painted furniture of the contemporary Viennese artist, Franz West. You said in your case the chair was much more considered as a chair. Later on I thought, yes, but your Abstract-Expressionist-style painting is much more decorative than Abstract Expressionism should be. Then I thought that actually in Franz West's case, that's the same too. But he has a different rationale than yours: you're respecting the thing that a chair must be, which might include being decorated. While he's respecting a kind of law of Conceptual Art, which says that you must step back from the heavy ineffable meanings that Abstract Expressionism is supposed to have. In a way, he has a sincere relationship to Conceptual Art – which is often an ironic type of style – so his use of a splashy mark might be ironic but it's is somehow still in a respectable art context. While with you, you remain in a design context. We're looking at something frankly decorative for decoration's sake, which in art would be like the plague.

Arad

Sure. I mean, it would, but I sort of claim a holiday from having to deal with any of this because – and I have a very good alibi here – because I'm not painting a chair. In both the series I showed you it wasn't like, 'Here's a chair and it's made now, and then here's a brush and some wonderful colours and let's go wild'. The paint and the colour are the raw material of these chairs. You can look at it without knowing all that, or without wanting to know all that, and you can see a decorated chair. But that's not my problem. I enjoy the freedom to suit myself and play. And I have a sort of mould – both a real one for the making of the chair, and in a way a metaphoric mould – that takes everything that I do and turns it into something else that's also a safe bet.

Collings

You mean a mental framework?

Arad

Yes, with whatever I do. And in this case I'm not painting, I'm just building the chair and it's made out of coloured polyester. I don't have to account for that surface in the same way as someone painting on canvas. I'm free from all that. Actually the same piece – the Big Easy – was accused of being sculpture before: designers dismiss it as, 'Ah, but this is sculpture, this is art'. While people who love it, praise it by saying, 'Ah, it's not a chair, it's not design – this is art'. And then weirdly, people from the art world can accept it with the thought, 'Ooh, I love your chair. Because I don't really think it's art'. They mean there's no threat there: you know – it can be polished stainless steel and it can reflect the world and whatever, and it has a shape, and they can say it reminds them a bit of Jean Arp, or whatever, but they can live with it. They can afford to love it unreservedly because it's in another field.

Collings

I suppose so. Maybe that's why I liked them all.

Welding, polishing and the decorative

Collings

Can you cast a bit more light on this problem of the decorative by talking about the development of your chairs after the Rover stage and the scaffolding stage?

Arad

There was part one and part two, and part one was the crude part. It was just a shape.

Collings

What do you mean 'crude'?

Opposite

Making a volume piece at the One Off workshop in 1989. The shape of a piece was drawn directly onto the steel, without any blueprint, then cut out and welded.

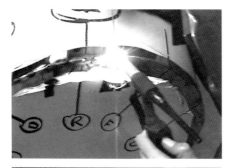

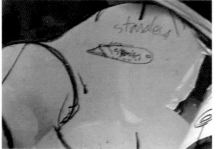

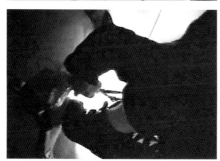

Arad

Well, I didn't know how to weld. I did some sketches – ten different things, and I thought, 'OK, I'll go ahead and do each one of them'. I thought, 'Let's do some pieces that don't go through this refining process that kills the directness of the sketch – can we do furniture that's like sketches? Because all I could do was sketch. I couldn't do really serious technical welding. So in my mind there was really just a piece of paper – only in reality it wasn't paper but steel. And I drew with a spray because that's more fluid, there's no friction. It's almost like graffiti. Buzz buzz! Then you take the shears, electric shears – and you cut it. Snip snip! And then you put all the skins together, all the envelopes, and tuck them with spot welding so the thing stands on the floor. And then you look at it and you change it a bit. You can bend it. Steel is actually a very forgiving material. It's not like wood, for which you really do have to be a craftsman. I mean, I always thought being a craftsman – well, I never wanted to be one. No patience. And then you start welding the line like that, and it's very crude...

Collings

You're soldering the bits together?

Arad

Yes. And there are photographs of me with a welding device but I didn't personally do a lot of it, really.

Collings

So the image of you as a heavy metal welder in the late 80s is a misconception.

Arad

It is, but it's like when you have snapshot of Lady Di – well, that's how you remember her.

Collings

Simpering – kind of a monster?

Arad

I mean a reduction. The photographer had twenty-four other pictures on the roll but the one we used was me welding. Anyway, I had people around me that time. And they learned to weld with me, except they got much better at it, and I never did. You know, when you weld, you see everything through black. You only see the point you're working on. And the strain is terrible, the pressure. It gives you a really hard time. Mostly I was the sighted person. So, anyway, this chair I was working on was sort of paraphrasing an overstuffed club chair. And it had a bit of Mickey Mouse, the ears, and a bit of some other kinds of shapes. And I used to say that, you know, the lines of the weld are the 'freehand', they're like the piping – and that's the drawing. Then we met some guy from up North who taught us that we can weld much more smoothly, that we can polish off the welding lines, and get rid of them altogether. So then polishing became a religion.

D-Sofa

1994
Mirror-polished stainless steel
Edition of 20
One Off

The D-Sofa was the last piece to be made in
the One Off London workshop before it was
relocated to Italy. 'This piece reflected the
transformation of our production and finishing
skills from crude to "state of the art". We were
dangerously close to becoming craftspeople.
D-Sofa is more of a virtuoso piece than the
earlier volume pieces.'

Big Easy 2 for 2
Sofa
1989
Mirror-polished stainless steel
Edition of 20
One Off

'This was a late evolution of the Big Easy.
Whereas the early Big Easys were about
crudeness and sketchiness, the later ones
were about finesse.'

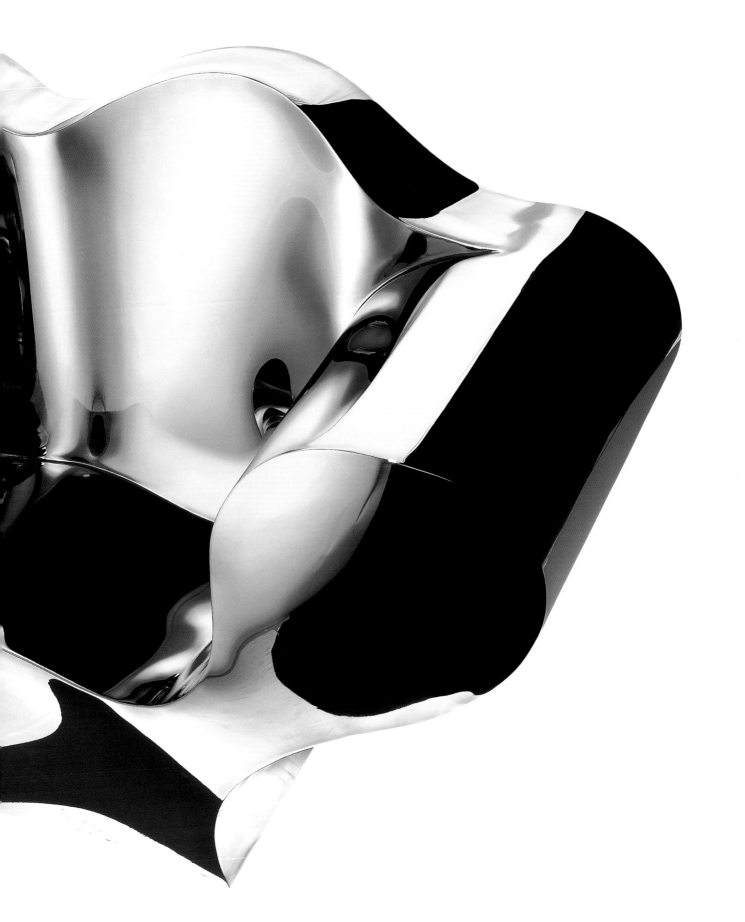

Collings

So that was part two: polishing.

Arad

Yeah. But in the crude stage I was the best with a hammer in my team. I always have to have something I'm better at than them. But with this welding and polishing, a whole demographic change came about in the workshop, because suddenly now it was full of refugees from art schools.

Collings

You're still in Covent Garden at this stage?

Arad

Yes, but also in Holborn, in Northington Street. We'd taken that on now, as well. And now the people working with me were new personalities: they were welders. And there was Rachel the Welder and Shaun the Welder. And they lived with the jargon of technical stuff, which made them very happy, and which I wasn't so good at. 'Have you T-20'd it?' You know, like...

Collings

And you wouldn't know if you had or not.

Arad

I wouldn't! So the first part is the crude part, where things like the Tinker Chair feature. But then pieces got more and more refined. And in this second part the whole new thing was that, you know, there is this piece of volume...

Right
Rachel Reynolds welding in the studios at Chalk Farm in 1989.

Opposite
Baby BOOPs
Bowls
2001
Stainless steel
Alessi

'Here, we lilliputted the gigantic aluminium bowls from the original BOOPs (Blown Out Of Proportion) series to make snack bowls. The miniaturisation of the form made these almost function-free pieces into useful products.' (Montage produced for 'Taking Liberties', an exhibition of Ron's work held at the Centre Santa Monica, Barcelona in 2003.)

Baby B.O.O.P'S

B.O.O.p's (blown out of proportion) is a collection of over-sized bowls, & vases of superplastic aluminium, formed in high temperature by air pressure, the shapes blown through a steel template, are mathematically organic. the original B.O.O.p's were deliberately very big to enjoy the full potential of the material and the process, making miniature version of the sculptural B.O.O.P's made the typology functional. alessi Baby BOOP are not blown & are not at all out of proportion they just borrowed the forms from

from blown aluminium
to pressed stainless steel
from sculptural to functional

Collings

Yes?

Arad

And it's like an enlarged piece of jewellery. So now we're going for completely smooth, whereas, before – when we were direct and primal – it was kind of action designing.

Collings

Now it's about finesse?

Arad

That's right. And later, just at the point where we thought we were really too committed to welding, or too committed to this metal workshop – well, that's when we closed the workshop. And we moved it to Italy. We started a place called Ron Arad Studio in collaboration with an Italian fabricator. It's in the north of Italy. And we, with them, went on doing this type of work. I used to go and visit, and instruct and supervise the making of the pieces. Collectors will sometimes tell you that a piece that was done here in Chalk Farm, where we're talking now – the studio here – is much more valuable than a piece that was done in Italy. Although there shouldn't be a difference and they were both numbered and signed and so on and so on forth.

Collings

How does this relate to the problem of the decorative? You're building up to it, right?

Arad

I think I am, if I remember what…oh yes, so the limited edition started to run out. There were lots of types, and pieces started to run out, but the demand for pieces went on. So I thought, with this particular piece, the Big

Previous
Two vases from BOOPs series
1998
Superplastic aluminium
Ongoing series of one-off pieces
The Gallery Mourmans

'This piece is part of the BOOPs (Blown Out Of Proportion) collection, a series borne out of discovering the possibilities of cavity-forming with superplastic aluminium. Plates of aluminium are inflated via air pressure through huge steel stencils, resulting in soft landscapes that are then cut and reassembled to form different large-scale objects.'

Right and opposite
Rolling Volume
Chair
1989
(Left) mild-steel, lead ballast; (right) mirror-polished stainless steel, lead ballast
Edition of 20 in each material
One Off

'This volume piece touches the floor at a tangent because its rear is heavily weighted with lead ballast. The weight tips it upwards, altering the conventional sitting and rocking action of this kind of chair – the sitter 'plays' against an invisible weight.'

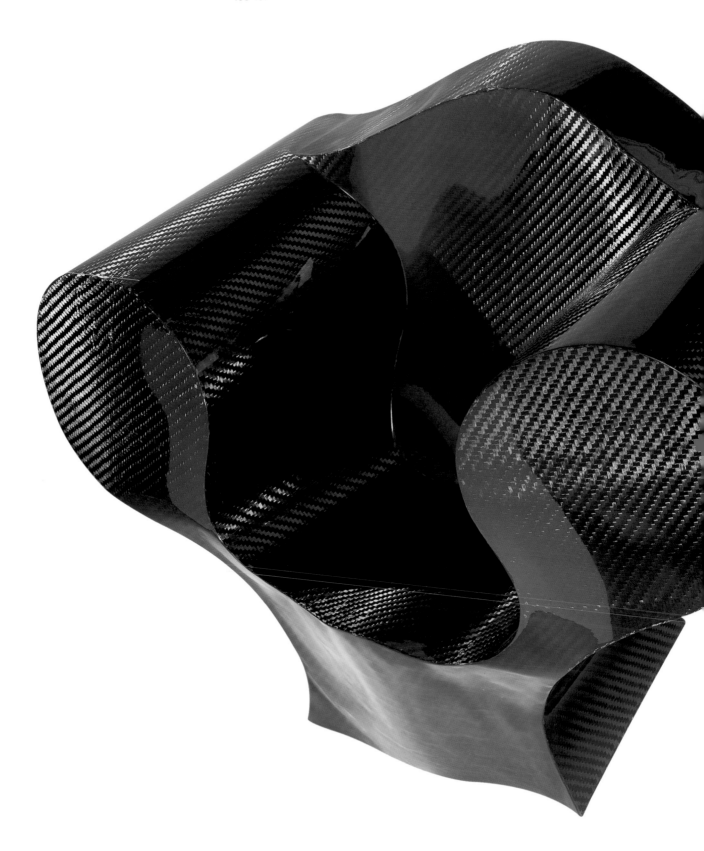

Carbon Fibre Big Easy
Chair
2002
Pre-peg wide-weave carbon fibre
Edition of 20
The Gallery Mourmans

The metal Big Easy evolved from the rough first
beginning to the jewel-like polished stainless
steel. The shape of the last stainless Big Easy of
the edition was cloned, first for the New Orleans
and secondly for this ultra lightweight carbon
fibre series.

Easy, I'll use the last one that was here. Look at this one, here in the studio
and you'll see what I mean, it's the last one that was made. Professional
metalworkers looked at it and wondered – 'How do you do it?' Because it's
totally seamless and perfect – maybe there's a bit of imperfection at this
point, but that used to be my trademark: a bit of imperfection.

Collings

What's imperfect about that?

Arad

Well, on that surface you see the reflection is not as smooth.

Collings

Oh, I see, yes. You think it's heavy but it's hollow: it's fake, it's a fake
volume. It's an air container, right? This one is a carbon-fibre Big Easy and
that one over there is the carbon-fibre Little Heavy. But this is a clone and
these are, like, a one-finger number.

Collings

Oh, that's great, you're picking it right up just with one finger.

Arad

Yes. My little finger. They are clones. The shape of this Big Easy is absolutely
identical to this Big Easy, because we used the stainless steel Big Easy to
make the mould for the carbon-fibre Big Easy. So that's also what I resorted
to when I went to New Orleans earlier. I resorted to the painted ones
because the metal ones were sold out, because we weren't allowed to make
another one. The last New Orleans I made I wrote 'Absolutely not for sale'
on it – and of course that's the one that people want to buy. This has
nothing to do with me physically doing it. It has something to do with me
wanting it. I recently saw one of my first Big Easys in Chicago, and I was
horrified to see how primitive it was.

Collings

You found it to be unacceptably crude?

Arad

Yes, and in a funny way it reminded me of fakes we sometimes see. And
ugly copies – well, there're quite a lot of them.

Collings

Really? So people actually pirate you?

Arad

They do, yes, and of course it's usually all wrong. And you can't sit on
them, and you can't look at them. But the one in Chicago...

Collings

That one appeared to you as if it was one of those: a pirate, a fake? But in
fact it was your own work, it was just that in the process of doing the next
forty after that first one, you'd become that much slicker?

Arad

Yeah, plus I suppose something in the air had changed slightly, too. You
know the story of Charlie Chaplin entering a Charlie Chaplin lookalike

contest, and coming second? It was like that, in a way. But going back to this whole decorative problem, which relates to the art problem – art and design, the essential and the inessential – well, what I've been saying is that I had those same discussions when I did these chairs. You know, as I said already, people would congratulate themselves on seeing the early chairs in a certain way: 'Ooh, it's sculpture', they'd say.

Collings

Right.

Arad

But then some people didn't like that idea, and they'd say, 'Hm, this isn't what sculpture's about!' And then, as I say, some people could afford to like it, precisely because it's not sculpture, and so it's not threatening to them. So, it was always there, this dispute: 'Is it art or is it design?' But it wasn't something that ever bothered me, not for a second. And so it wasn't a big headache for me when I started painting, either – when I started painting these chairs. I wasn't actually painting a surface, as I've already explained, but that wasn't a great cause of celebration for me – you know, 'Wow, I've by-passed a problem of art!' I was just building something out of colour. I noticed the same thing in Marc Quinn's sculptures recently, and I liked it when he did that. You know, when he's just pouring coloured stuff. I can get into that and I can see what he's doing. There's a sort of excitement of doing something new, something that wasn't done before. It's not just…

Collings

New in a technical sense…?

Arad

In any sense – I don't care where newness comes from. As long as it's not just, 'Yes, I'm joining the conversation. Yes, I'm joining the jargon. Yes, I can do that as well. And I can do it maybe a little better'. So, I liked the pleasure of being able to paint, without putting on painter's overalls and saying, 'Ah yes, I'm painting now'. I was just building something, and that gave me a bit of freedom from worry, or freedom from doing something inhibited.

Collings

And did you feel you were testing your audience: they might not like what you were doing?

Arad

I have to say that in this series there was absolutely no risk like that at all. Maybe it's a bad thing, but really with everything I did there was never any danger of it staying put…

Collings

Of not selling?

Arad

Yes, it was a game, and because of that it was free – that's part of the lifting of inhibition.

Carbon Little Heavy
Chair
2001
Carbon-fibre
Edition of 20
The Gallery Mourmans

'This is a clone of the Little Heavy, an earlier volume piece made in steel. It's ultra-light – it only weighs as much as a bag of sugar.'

Box in 4 movements

More decorative

Collings

I suppose the received idea that stands behind art people saying, 'Oh, horror – the decorative', is that 'the decorative' in this mindset is always an addition. It can be taken away. And when you take it away then there's the essence, revealed. The decorative is the excessive. So when we have the thought, 'We're dealing with the merely decorative here,' we know we're in a world of pointless flimflam, and we're supposed to resist that – we must be critical of the unimportant.

Arad

Right, yes. 'Decorative' when you paint it is to do with surface as well. And when I was painting, the thing was all about depth as well: I mean, you could see through layers. So with this sense of 'depth' the decoration became the material. It's just a simple descriptive thing I'm saying here. It's like looking at marbles. You know, like child's marbles. And maybe there's even a childish magpie pleasure to it.

Collings

It's amusing that we're on the edge of a discussion about the profound versus the unprofound, while we know perfectly well that most discussion within the contemporary art world about the profound is quite unprofound and just routine showing off. And really one could just as easily talk straightforwardly about the decorative as talk inanely about the profound. How do you think this idea of the decorative has changed for you over the years?

Arad

Well, you know, I showed you that container – that's what I'd call that chair shape: it's a container, really. I showed you my ugliest one and you didn't see it as ugly. Because that container was such a brilliant container it could take anything! But there's another more horrific stage to all this that we haven't mentioned yet: there's the comfortable.

Collings

Phew! Even more terrifying!

Previous
Box in Four Movements
Chair
1994
Stainless steel
Edition of 20
Ron Arad Studio, Italy

'Probably our favourite piece. It's easy to read as a versatile object – you can easily imagine different configurations, but the suppleness provided by the torsion springs is a surprise you enjoy only when you attempt to sit on it.'

Left
Box in Four Movements
1994

'Sketches of this piece were almost like typography – I drew them non-stop. There must have been hundreds of permutations.'

7
Chairs get industrial treatment
Playful
Early chairs
Vases, sculptures, computers

Chairs get industrial treatment

Collings

I know how art is made. Tell me more about how chairs are made.

Arad

About two or three years after I made the Big Easy I made another version, which we took to Milan. We go to Milan every year to do a gallery show as well as to launch designs we have done for other companies. Anyway, this version was really the same as the Big Easy but just an inch smaller in every dimension. I had covered it with an inch of foam, and I had it upholstered in Kentish Town. At first it was a paraphrase of an overstuffed club chair. And then I made one in sort of red leatherette.

Collings

And that one got really close to an overstuffed club chair?

Arad

Yes, it became it. And when I took that to Milan I asked myself, 'What if people like it?' Because it's like after – you know – telling them that you can make chairs out of metal, and so on and so forth, all of sudden I do this reversal. Although in fact it was more expensive to make than the metal chair, because first I had to make the chair, and only afterwards cover it. So I was completing the cycle of making a stuffed club chair once again, that was soft or softer, but still heavy because inside there was the real thing, the metal thing. And how about even the price making a statement? How to make the price say something? Let's make it even cheaper. I don't know …I just wanted to see what would happen, and I'm not sure I really had any particular results in mind. I mean, I wasn't sure if I wanted people to be appalled by it.

Collings

Maybe there was a hint of conservatism about it, so the price being lower might balance that with a bit of radicalism?

Arad

In any case, an Italian company called Moroso approached me. They did

Plastic Little Albert
Chair
2001
Rotation-moulded polyethelene
Moroso

The rotation-moulding machine used to produce the chair

upholstered furniture. In fact they actually made the chair you are sitting on now. They're a typical Italian family business, where the father is second generation. They made upholstered things for years, but then they made a mistake and sent Patrizia, the daughter, to University of Bologna, and she comes back a different person – now she wants to change the company. She hangs out with radicals and she's married to a guy who does cartoons, or comics, or something. Anyway, she actually really does turn the company around, and today it's one of the leading names in contemporary design, very successful. So she saw this chair and she asked, 'Can we produce it?' I say, 'Yes, OK.' So the initial things were copies of metal pieces. And if you look at the screen now, you'll see how the chairs done by Moroso were initially cut by a computer. And you see that thing in the middle is a skeleton to

Collings

Yes?

Arad

Well, you take that out and you put the skeleton in and...

Collings

What exactly are we looking at? Is that a mould?

Arad

No. This is a lump of foam. If it were Michelangelo it would be a lump of marble, yes?

Collings

Of course!

Arad

We could talk about that later: the four ways of making something. One of them is called 'wasting'. You know, as if there's a statue inside a lump of foam.

Collings

You mean, like the lost wax process in casting?

Arad

Lost wax is something else.

Collings

Oh, OK.

Arad

That's casting and moulding.

Collings

Well, let's not go too far, because remember – I don't know anything.

Arad

Look, here's an image on the screen of a double Big Easy – it's the Big Easy doubled, but also soft, upholstered and lighter. And affordable.

Collings

And it's leather?

Arad

You can choose. Moroso have millions of swatches and you can order it to

Soft Big Easy
Chair
1990
Polyurethane foam
Moroso

Ron with a scale model of the Soft Big Easy and a block of foam illustrating how the automatic cutting process used to make the chair begins. 'This is the real-world, mass-production version of the Big Easy: cheaper, lighter, softer, and coming in different sizes and colours – even in a children's version! What started as a metal paraphrase of an over-stuffed club chair ended up as an over-stuffed club chair.'

Victoria & Albert Sofa

2000

Polyeurethane, fibreglass, upholstery

Moroso

As this montage (produced for 'Taking Liberties', an exhibition of Ron's work held at the Centre Santa Monica, Barcelona in 2003) explains, the looped core of the Victoria & Albert sofa was originally going to be made from tempered steel, but the final design used fibreglass.

match your trousers if you want. But it became a real piece of furniture. And this is a pattern you find now in lots of things I do: they start as studio pieces and they become industrialized. But this was the first attempt. It was as if some Japanese people came with their cameras to our studio, went back to Tokyo and said, 'Right, OK – let's do the copies'. Except I'm the Japanese guy.

Collings

What else did Moroso produce?

Arad

Here's another one on the screen. This one I did as a joke. I called it Heart and Industry. It's full of lead here, in the tail – it makes it rock in a very nice way. I made it in steel and it's a very tongue-in-cheek piece. Can you imagine this reflective and convex and extremely comfortable? We produced the

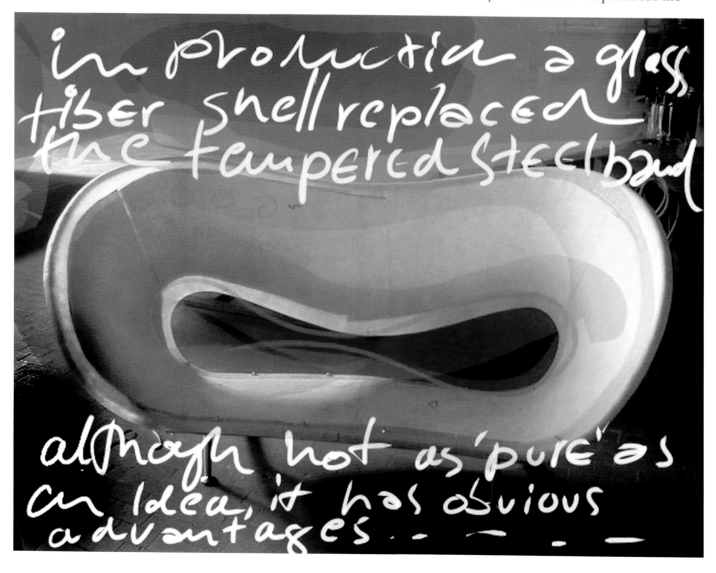

in production a glass fiber shell replaced the tempered steel band

although not as 'pure' as an idea, it has obvious advantages.. – - - _ _

Soft Heart for Moroso and to my horror, for a while, it was the best selling piece of the Spring Collection. I couldn't make enough of them. And I never intended it as a serious piece. It's a little exercise in making whatever you want, and not worrying too much about it. There were things I liked in the Spring Collection – for example, there's the spring in this one, and instead of having rockers on a straight floor I made a curved plinth, so it's called Chair on a Pedestal. Because I don't like the fact that when you do an exhibition of chairs people put them on pedestals, so I thought this one would be immune because it had its own pedestal. And again it has its own action: you can see that it's a rocker.

Collings

You can rock on a pedestal?

Arad

Yeah. And this one you might have seen at my house. It's called Tilt. And this one, the Big Easy, was once crude like a sketch, and then refined, and then built in colours. And before an upholstered version...back to normal, as if the chair is saying, 'I can be normal as well'.

Collings

It's playing with ideas of the normal versus the strange, the excessive versus the cut back?

Arad

Yes, all that. And the double one is now found in the receptions of big advertising companies, as well as in homes. And then there's the children's version. And it's been done in metal, carbon fibre, plastic and leather. And

Right
Soft Heart
Chair
1990
Upholstered polyurethane foam, lead ballast
Moroso

'I wasn't that pleased when what was a tongue-in-cheek piece became the best-selling piece of Moroso's Spring Collection. What was tongue-in-cheek about it? People loved it.'

Opposite
Plastic Little Albert
Chair
2001
Rotation-moulded polyethelene
Moroso

Removing the chair from its mould.

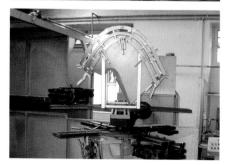

now as we're speaking, what's happening with it is this: the rotation moulding version: there's going to be a cheap, cheap, cheap version of this chair done with this technique.

Collings

You said earlier that the chair is just a container – it can be done any way?

Arad

Yes. In the rotation moulded version there's a cavity, there's the shape of the mould and there's the granules of plastic. It gets heated and the inside goes molten. And then it's rotated – right? – like a shaker on the bar. And you can paint the mould.

Collings

So these ones we're sitting in, now, these ones you call the Little Albert, the rotation mould technique you used for these is going to be used for these new ones you're now talking about?

Arad

Yeah, it's a technique favoured by young designers. Do you know Tom Dixon? He's now the creative director of Habitat.

Collings

He was a designer name in the late 80s, wasn't he?

Arad

Yes. He was one of the first to start working in rotation moulding. He called it tooling. It's the cheapest way to do something in plastic. But it's very slow, they can only make twenty-five chairs out of one mould per day. But young designers wouldn't sell that much anyway, so it sort of suits them. But I think a lot of credit should be given to Tom. I think he was the first one to sort of play with that rotation mould technique. I can see you don't know what I'm talking about, but it's the same technique they use for making bollards in the street. And for dispensers for free Australian newspapers. That's why the material must be cheap. So it is cheap. America is full of them.

Collings

So a lot of American crap is made of that?

Arad

Yes. So looking at the computer screen again, you can see here the machine that does rotation moulding. Here it is rotating, and making a Little Albert. This is the factory that now does rotation moulding for everyone. It's almost like Adidas and Nike. Those two companies do timesharing in the same factory in the Far East. You know – their products are made by the same people.

Collings

For all the design companies – for Nike?

Arad

Yes. On the inside there is this chair like a cake. And you take it out. It's so simple: it's a very primitive way of doing something in plastic. And we're

Little Albert
Chair
2000
Upholstered polyurethane foam
Moroso

'Little Albert is the latest addition to the Victoria &
Albert Collection – all the pieces centred on the
idea of a continuous loop of foam. Although Little
Albert inherits something from its predecessors,
it doesn't follow the loopy rules religiously.'

Right
Plastic Little Albert
Chair
2001
Rotation-moulded polyethelene
Moroso

'The shape of the upholstered Little Albert lent itself to a rota-mould version. The fact that it is a largely tapered shape means that it can be made using a mould in just two parts, and can be removed really easily.'

Below
Nino Rota
Chair
2002
Rotation-moulded polyethelene
Cappellini

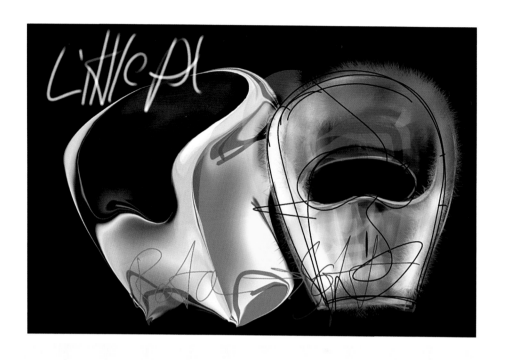

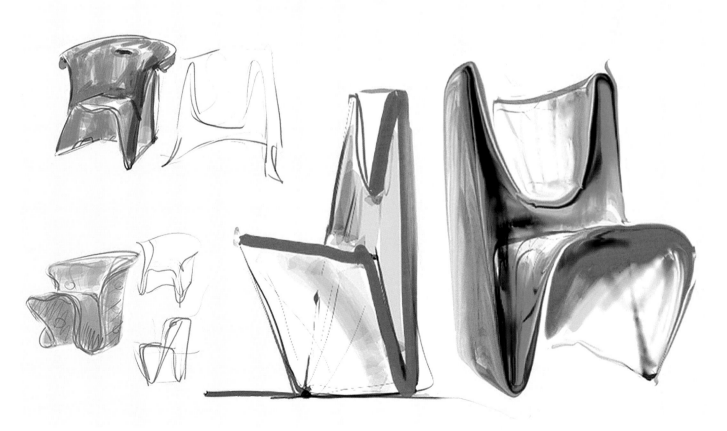

Nino Rota
Chair
2002
Rotation-moulded polyethelene
Cappellini

'It seemed a good idea to mould a pair of chairs
in one go, later splitting the moulded piece into
two identical twins. The intention was to double
the production capacity of the slow rota-
moulding process. We now know that all the
advantages of two-in-one are wiped out by the
necessity of having to get another set of
machinery to split them. However, this
miscalculation resulted in a chair that probably
would never otherwise have been designed.'

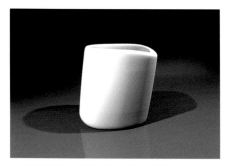

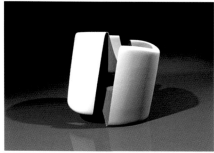

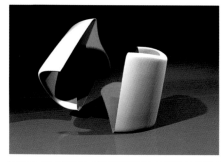

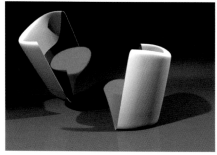

talking about it now because the Big Easy is about to get the same treatment. And once again, it's from the studio pieces to mass production.

Collings

Will it sell in Habitat?

Arad

No, in furniture shops, where these kinds of things sell.

Collings

So the more fancy metal things are not in furniture shops, but these Little Albert plastic ones are?

Arad

Yes. And there'll be distribution all over the world. These companies have agents and area managers and – it's a whole industry. But furniture's not as big as the fashion industry, of course. I mean, you can see it in the papers: they're full of the fashion reports from the fashion shows in Milan and Paris, with the same photo every day. But there's relatively little about design. Yes, there will be the one article about the Milan furniture show by someone who has hardly visited anything. But, well, furniture's still small in relation to fashion.

Playful

Collings

In all this talk about the way this chair has mutated, and all the things that have developed out of it, the theme is playfulness?

Arad

Yes.

Collings

And you apply all your seriousness and effort, that is, all your ideas and your energies, to doing something basically playful and entertaining?

Arad

Yes. And here's some more of that on the screen now...

Collings

We're looking at an animation of a sort of biomorphic thing. The foam one looks quite good.

Arad

It's excellent! But let me show you something else. Almost like a pop video of making the stuff.

Collings

It's a film of you and some guys making the chairs, with a music soundtrack...

Arad

Yes, it was made by some Italian film-makers. This guy you see now, he's retired, but he comes for a session every time I go to this place – it's near Venice. And he's Michelangelo with the knife.

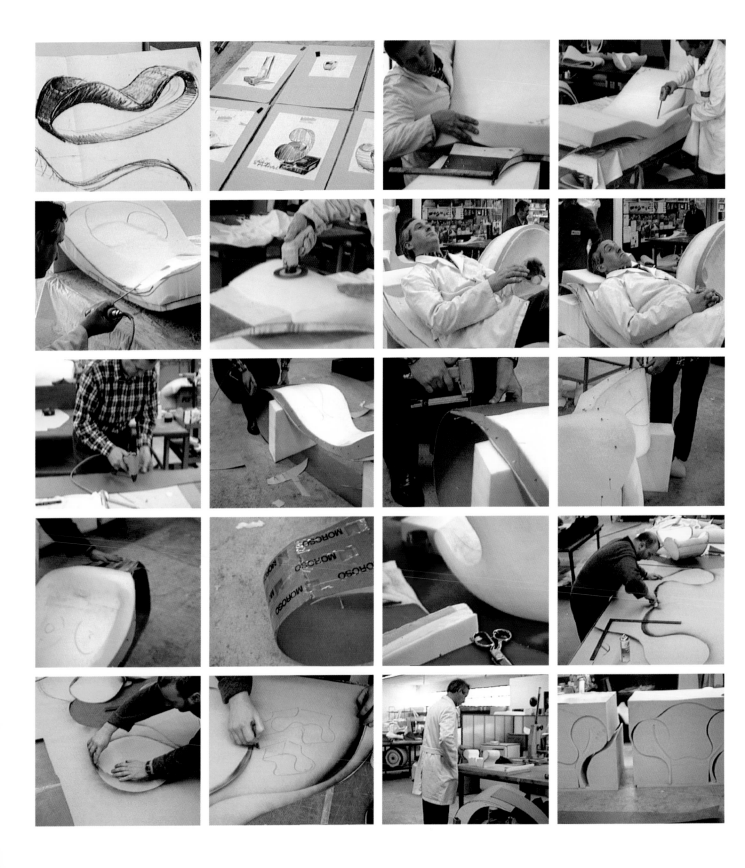

Collings

He comes out of retirement to do this?

Arad

Yeah, he's called Uncle Marino: he comes to work with me because it's easier for me to work with him than with anybody else, even though he doesn't speak English. In this image I'm saying, 'Let's shape it a bit here'.. And look, it's like stone.

Collings

We're looking at a lot of different textures now.

Arad

Well, we're making the types now, and each is slightly different. And we choose and then there's a mould made for it. We don't cut them every time.

Collings

How many different types are there so far?

Arad

About five or six in this collection.

Collings

Presumably Patrizia at Moroso has her own idea of what 'radical' is?

Arad

Yes, the company has its own agenda, of course. It's not the same as my agenda because they're bigger. They're running a factory with hundreds of people working there. They need to pay them, and they need to make money. It's a commercial thing for them. And sometimes it suits a company to be radical or to be different to everyone else, because everyone gets too similar.

Collings

Yes, but that doesn't make them the Red Brigade.

Arad

Well, the thing is, this is a field in which it does make sense to talk about being radical, but you have to see it all through different glasses than you're used to. This is really the very trendy, high end of furniture. That is one arena. But then of course there is our yearly show at Marconi Gallery in Milan.

Collings

I know that place! In fact, weirdly, I once exhibited there, in a group show organised by Liam Gillick. So you're designing for different furniture companies in Milan and at the same time you have a show every year at Marconi.

Arad

Every year in April, in Milan, it's the furniture fair, and my show at Marconi coincides with that. So one year my show at Marconi was called, 'Not made by hand, not made in China. It was about growing computer-generated objects in tanks. Another year it might be about inflated aluminium or maybe composite paper.

'Prototyping pieces for mass production requires skilled artisans. These images of us making prototypes feature Uncle Marino (I don't know his surname – everyone just calls him Uncle Marino), a wonderful man who retired from Moroso a number of years ago, but who returns to join us in every project that we do with the company.'

Beware of the Dog
Daybed
1990
Mild steel, tempered steel
Edition of 20
Ron Arad Associates

'A loop, half of it a rigid double skin of boxed mild
steel, the other half a single line of tempered steel.
The rigid shape is predetermined (designed
around the body), and the sprung shape is natural
and harmonic. Lying on it reminds a lot of people
of bobbing in a small boat.'

Right
Tinker Chair
1988
Mild steel, stainless steel
Edition of 6
One Off

'These chairs are made from sheet steel that is beaten to death with a rubber mallet until it confesses to being a chair. The torture continues until there is a consensus among trial sitters that it is a very comfortable chair. At this point, its two sides are welded on and the shape is fixed. The first two chairs had the joy of discovery in them; the third and fourth were OK; but the fifth one felt like it was copying its predecessor – so there was no sixth.'

Below
IPCO
Light
2001
Glass fibre, polyester, tungsten bulb
Edition of 50
The Gallery Mourmans

'The IPCO (Inverted Pinhole Camera Obscura) light throws out a multi-directional projection of the filament of a single light bulb. We made some customised bulbs where the filaments spelt words like 'yes', 'no' and 'maybe', but they didn't last long – Edison's bulbs needed no improvement.'

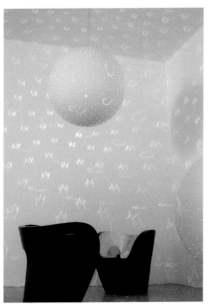

Collings

Is the atmosphere usually very different at these different types of shows?

Arad

Actually there's a big overlap, and a lot of cross-fertilizing. I mean, whereas I just fought with you a bit over the art camp and the design camp – in Milan they know: Milan knows it needs a tonic. Or it needs teasing. It needs excitement. And actually they should give us a grant in the name of that tonic. I can't really not do Milan, but it's always a temptation to have a rest.

Collings

Do you ever not show any furniture at these Marconi shows?

Arad

Well, here's something I did there.

Collings

This looks like an art installation. It's got a sort of light going around. It looks like a joke on a mirror ball.

Arad

It's serious. It's not a joke. It's an IPCO, a reversed camera obscura. So every pinhole, in a way, is a camera. And that's what you see: a filament.

That is, the Edison Filament. Before, we worked really hard on getting the filaments to say things like, 'Yes', 'No', or 'Maybe'. And we had, like, dissolve units. So, in the room it said, 'Yes', 'No', 'Maybe', etc. But none of the bulbs lasted very long, because they were too handmade. So then I decided there's nothing wrong with the light bulb as Edison did it. We can invent our own way of writing with light…this is the Ballpark: so you see the word 'light' written with the balls, reflecting the word 'dark' on the wall – you can change the words endlessly. When we showed it in Tokyo it said 'God'. And then the reflection spelt 'War'.

Collings

Right.

Arad

Not only that. I put a slide in the source of the light so you could see Osama Bin Laden in every ball. It's just an idea – you have it, you act it out. And what you're looking at now on the screen is a little ball out of a mouse – you know: the mouse for a computer. I planted a little mirror in each one of them. And this is like a bed of nails, but with computer-mouse eyeballs instead of nails. You can direct any of them to wherever you want. And you can make them spell out whatever you want. 'Happy Birthday', if you like – whatever. So it is…I don't know where to place this. It's not a functional object and it's not a light. So I don't know what it is, it's just there. And one year my Marconi show would look like that, but last year it was more back to furniture.

Early chairs

Collings

What are these images we're looking at now, on the computer?

Arad

We're looking at the Tinker Chairs. These are, well, they're what I could do in those days. I didn't know any better. And that's the rubber hammer. It was like improvising – just hitting steel with a hammer, and hitting it and hitting it, until everyone around you says, 'Yeah it's comfortable but…' Then you just make it provide a little bit more support on the lower back: 'OK, hang on', you say. And then when you weld the sides, it fixes it and it becomes like a solid container.

Collings

When did you do those?

Arad

Well, they're photographed on the site of what became the Millennium Dome, in Greenwich, and I remember that photo shoot – so it must have been the mid to late 1980s.

Collings

We're looking at Tinker Chairs out in a wasteland?

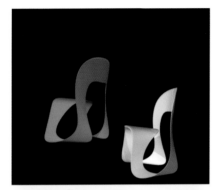
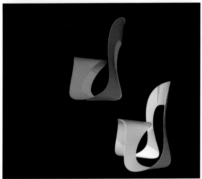
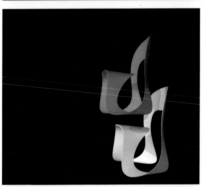
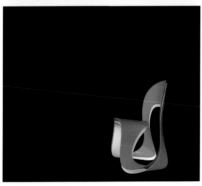

Arad

Yeah, the photographer decided to take the picture there. I did six of those chairs – they were very popular. People bought them. But by number six I couldn't do it any more. 'How am I going to it?' I thought – I wondered, 'How did I do it yesterday?'

Collings

So the moment passes?

Arad

And you get upset with the thing, because it's not as good as the earlier one. And you drop it. But it's the same even when you're much further on, and the technology is more sophisticated – like this Stacking Chair.

Collings

Ah, so this is a very different image on the screen now. It's something done with a sophisticated moulding process, or folding process, or something.

Arad

Well, first of all it's done on a computer.

Collings

So we've gone from hammered steel to computer generated forms.

Arad

Yeah, there's about twenty years between them. And still, there's the white one on the right and the red one on the left, and really nothing has changed. The height of the chair is the same, they both do their best to be comfortable. No one would know they come from the same source, but of course to me to me it's the same thing. Only the method of making is different.

Collings

Isn't that more or less everything?

Arad

No, the method is only part of it. It's not everything.

Collings

How would you sum up what connects the two over the twenty years?

Arad

The similarity is that they're both really plasticine – in effect: you work on them until you're happy. Until something in you says, 'Yes, this is it. You can stop now'. And of course you can always go on, but also the thing can curdle as well. Look over there at the other computers – there's some of my staff, working on screens. I used to think everything came from my pencil, now I think it's the screen. Every day the same thing: we move the line a little bit, improve it, we make changes no one else but us will ever know about.

Collings

So there are subtle nuances. You and the team see a form through all these tiny stages, over a long period?

Swan Chair
Work in progress
2001–2004
Plastic
Magis

'These early computer renderings of the Swan
Chair (a temporary nickname) show one of our
"slow developers" – very demanding on materials
and geometry. It's a one-band stacking chair
that also stacks sideways. The version shown
here is designed to be produced in plastic.'

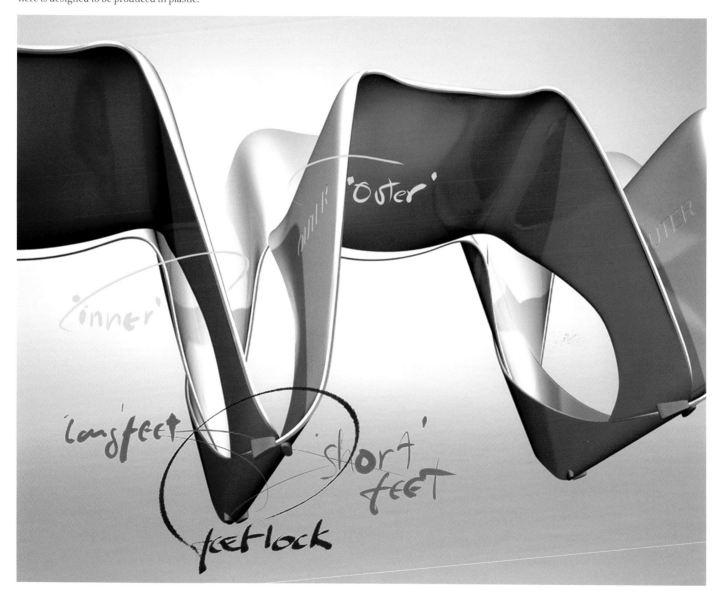

Swan Chair

2001–2004
Aluminium
Magis

'"Who needs another plastic chair?" In late
2003, we finally abandoned plastic in favour
of aluminium with gradual corrugations
reminiscent of the Tom Vac chair. But unlike the
Tom Vac, where the aluminium version was a
limited studio production, here it offers an
industrial solution.'

Arad

Yes, it can still go wrong, but the thing still starts out with an idea of how to impose your will.

Collings

I see. You're saying that with the first one we can see that it's a beaten-out thing, but with the recent ones we can't see they've gone through all that minute adjustment?

Arad

Yes. Actually the new one we're looking at now on the screen is never going to happen anyway.

Collings

Why?

Arad

Because the company that was going to make it was too slow off the mark, so I gave it to another company, and then in the meantime it changed.

Collings

Oh, so you already moved on? This prototype became passé for you? And these are the new ones: these white ones?

Arad

Yes, but they're still the same type. The only change is that it doesn't only stack upwards now, it also stacks sideways: as far as I know, no one did that before! Which is another source of pleasure. To design is also to do something that didn't exist before.

Collings

So now we've looked at two different types of chairs: the first beaten out ones from twenty years ago and now these new ones, which were computer generated. And earlier, we were looking at the painted ones from a few years ago.

Arad

The similarity between the painted one and the beaten up one is sort of the action painting element of it: you're there, the material is there. OK, a camera's there, also! But it's just like drawing or painting, and at the same time it's slightly different.

Collings

What about with the computer-generated one?

Arad

As we speak now, see Yuko's face there as she concentrates – she's still working on this, like she's been working every day for the last month. And every time I go from here past her there, I'll stop and talk about how it's going.

Collings

So that's the equivalent to the beating of the hammer?

Arad

Yes. But she's a better hammer than the hammer.

Ge-Off Sphere
2001
Light
Polyamide
The Gallery Mourmans

Many of Ron's recent designs are made by rapid prototyping. This process comprises taking a set of instructions from a computer-rendered 3-D model of an original design and sending them to another computer that controls a laser. This then either selectively cures resin (stereolithography) or fuses grains of polyamide powder (laser sintering), causing a piece to literally 'grow' in a tank. The pictures shows an early experimental epoxy resin version of the Ge-Off Sphere in the last stages of 'growing' in a tank. 'The final edition of 20 Ge-Offs were made in polyamide using the selective laser sintering process – the polyamide provided the flexibility the design required.'

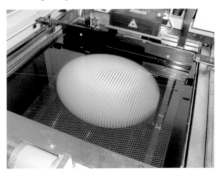

Vases, sculptures, computers

Collings

You were talking about computer screens.

Arad

Yes, nowadays everything I do starts out on the machines I have here and at home...

Collings

The sketch-pad programme?

Arad

Yeah, so a lot of things have changed – the method has changed.

Collings

Originally it was a basic scribble feel: drawing with a pencil, which included the utility feel, the functional feel and the feel of – well, what feels right.

Arad

Nowadays I've still got all that, but the advantage of computers is that when you're using the sketch-pad programme the canvas never dries. The models are so sophisticated now. So if I move something here, looking at the screen now, this would move on the other side. I don't have to do the adjustment myself. If you want something to stay symmetrical, well, you move one thing and it corrects everything else.

Collings

They're vases, right?

Arad

Yes. When you work in computers you see lots of wire frames. Are you familiar with those?

Collings

No.

Arad

Before a computer model is actually rendered there's an illusionistic wire frame. It's known only to whoever's working in front of the screen. It's conceptual only, it never existed off the screen and it never will exist – you've never seen a real one in your life. So I decided to give a thickness to every wire and to make the bars. But don't accuse me of making a sculpture. I'm a designer, right? I'm not a potter. So, we can send an email of this to a machine, and the next day DHL will give us the piece.

Collings

DHL will deliver the real thing made up from the computer design?

Arad

Yes. We'll send an email to Belgium and the piece will come back. It's still an expensive technique, though. And to make it saleable, or for the finances to work, you have to make it unique. So it says here, 'This is a

Vases

1999
Dyed polyamide (blue design)
Epoxy resin (white design)
Unique pieces
The Gallery Mourmans

This pair of images features the computer-rendered 3-D models of two vases, and the end result of 'growing' the final pieces in a tank, using stereolithography. 'These designs applied a pioneering use of rapid prototyping. Instead of treating the results of the process as templates for further design, we saw them as final objects.' The vases incorporate the sentence 'This is a unique piece, the computer file used to generate it was destroyed on the 18 March '99'.

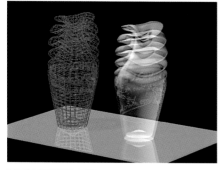

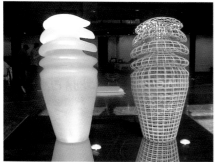

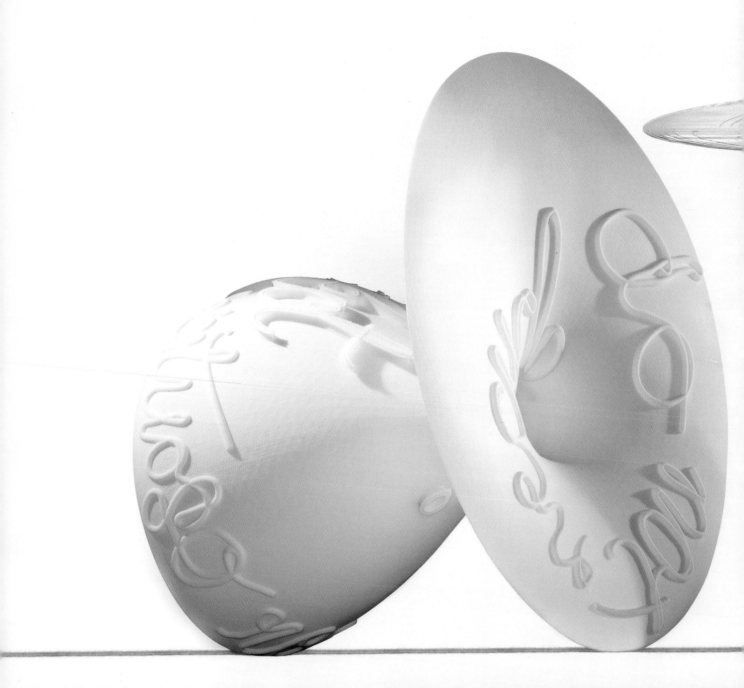

Perfect Vases

2001
Epoxy resin (left), polyamide (right)
Edition of 20
The Gallery Mourmans

Two pieces made using the rapid prototyping
process. 'After designing a number of very
laboured lights, and vases and bowls that
featured extruded handwriting, the Perfect
Vase is a quick 3-D sketch in one take, inscribed
in extruded lettering with the phrases/words
"virtuoso reality", "perfect" and "do not recycle".'

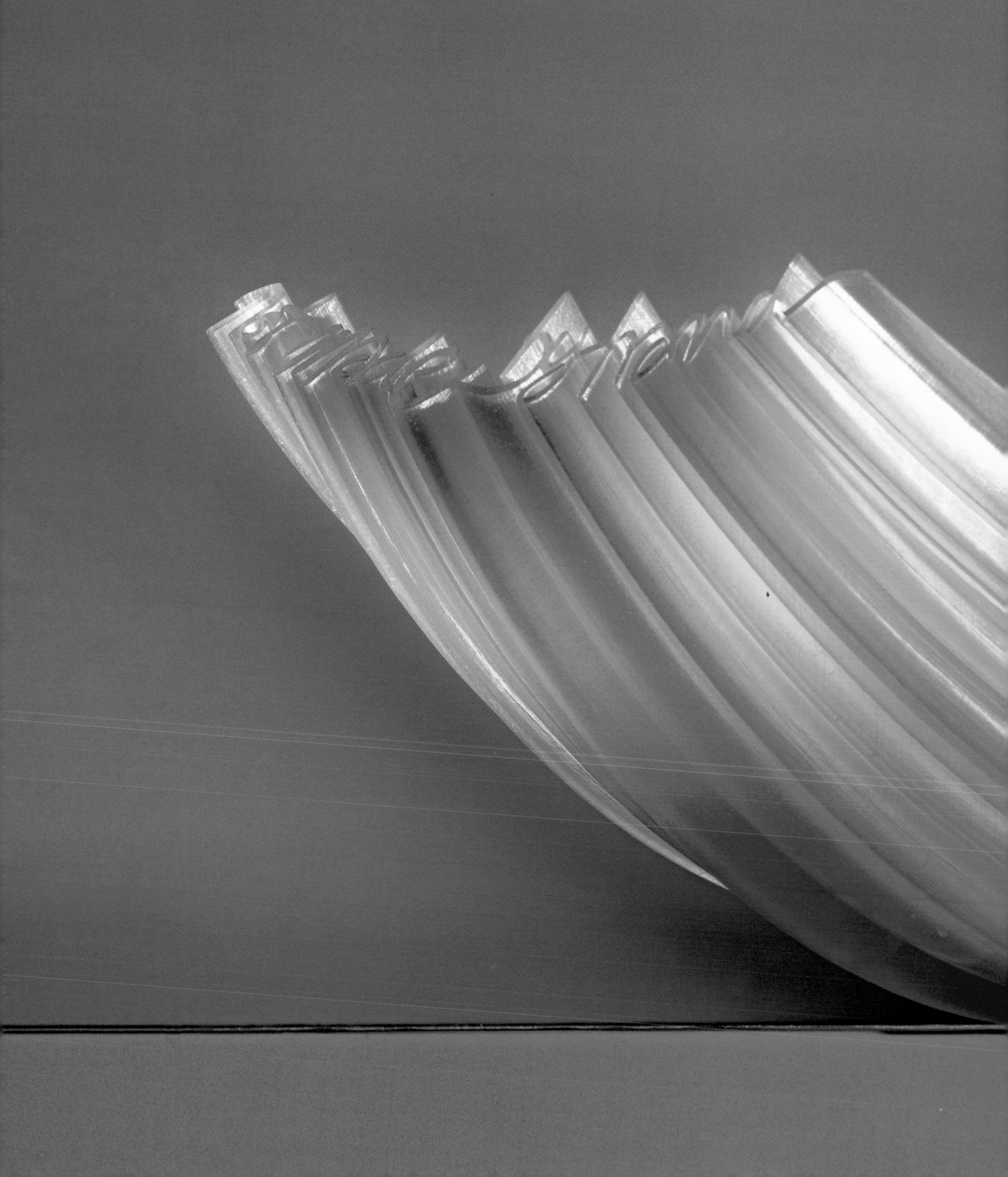

Not Made By Hand
Bowl
2001
Epoxy resin
Edition of 20
The Gallery Mourmans

Another piece made using the rapid prototyping
process. 'A sample of my handwriting – "Not
Made By Hand" – was extruded along a path of
changing scale to form a banana-shaped bowl.'

Bouncing Vases
2001
Polyamide
The Gallery Mourmans

'One of 160 frames of a computer-rendered animated 3-D model of my original design can be 'grown' to order using the selective laser sintering process. You can have anything from a compact bowl to one that is stretched to its fullest reach.'

Following pages
Hot Ingo (left), and **Hot Tango**
Lights
2001
Polyamide, stainless steel, halogen bulb, fluorescent ring
Edition of 20 of each
The Gallery Mourmans.

'One of these vases is named after Ingo Maurer, the other after Yuki Tango, who is head of our product design team. The vases we had been making were more of a research exercise, but these lights apply the discoveries that came out of that research – how you could rapid prototype final objects. The geometry and the material of the lights allow for an incredible flexibility.'

unique piece, the computer file used to generate this object was destroyed on 15 March 1999'.

Collings

It says it in a scribbled writing style.

Arad

The writing is the same thickness as the wire frame. And now here's a real one on the screen. If I remember right, this one says, 'On the 15 March, 1999, London'. That one went wrong. Here's another one.

Collings

Is it plastic?

Arad

Yes. In the making, no one touched it, right? It grew in a tank.

Collings

So you sent them a little email and they sent back this grown epoxy vase?

Arad

Yes. Or this one, this is polyamide, it's like nylon. And this is its original wire frame version: that one's spiritual and that one's real.

Collings

Great! So one was a virtual sort of diagram and then the next picture we saw was the real thing?

Arad

This is the model we send: it's not just a picture, it's a model, a computer model. And then that one's the real thing.

Collings

Yes, looking pretty much like the model.

Arad

Not pretty much – exactly. And here's another one but a different type. This one was made using a modelling technique that can only be done

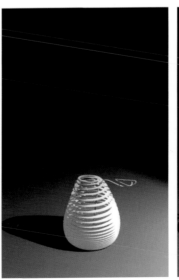

by computer, there's no other way it could be done, no artisan could attempt it.

Collings

We're looking at an image of a sort of swirling-shape vase that disappears into space.

Arad

Yes. And you animate it like this.

Collings

Now it's sort of breathing as we look at it, like a spring or a coil.

Arad

And if you were a collector and you said, 'I want to buy this one,' I'd have to say, 'I'm sorry it's sold, and there's no other like it'. But I would be able to say to you, 'How about a different frame?'

Collings

Do those industrial design companies come to you, or do you go to them?

Arad

Oh, well, it's not so simple. First of all I wasn't trained as an industrial designer – I was totally ignorant about the profession. I didn't know how industrial products and projects come into existence. It was never my intention to join the profession. But in any case I did a few things and then because of them, Vitra approached me. They thought there might be a link there with what they did. And that started a pattern of me originating industrial-design projects. So a lot of the stuff that was later translated into industrial production started off as studio pieces.

Collings

For example?

Arad

Well, take the Bookworm, which is the number-one bestseller that came

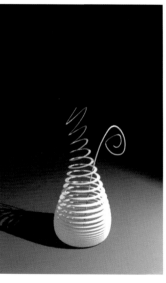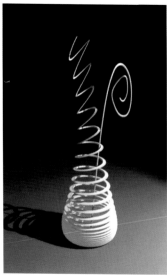

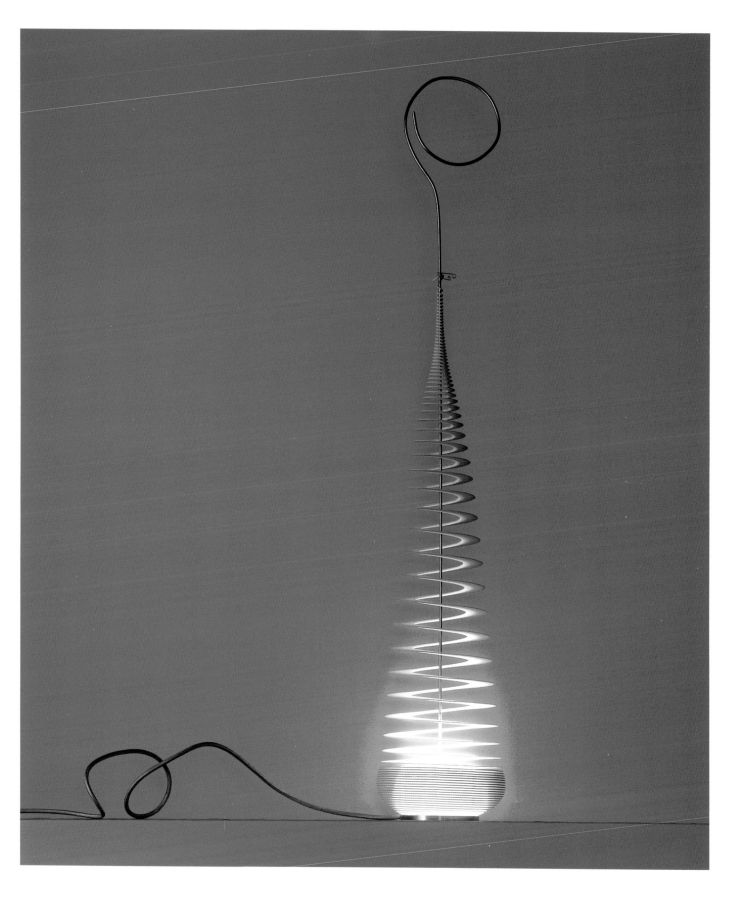

Topot
Outdoor plant pot
2002
Rotation-moulded polyethelene
Serralunga

'Rotation moulding is normally a 'cheap' and
'dumb' technique – this project pushes the
technology a bit further. The air-tight double
skin pot can be squeezed and fixed at different
heights by plugging the hole at the base of the
internal skin once you have the required
amount of air.'

Page 142
Photo-montage showing the flexible action

FPE
Chair
1997
Plastic, aluminium
Kartell

'With the FPE (Fantastic Plastic Elastic) chair, the
transparent plastic seat is inserted into double-
barrelled aluminium extrusions before bending.
When it's bent to shape, the extrusion bites the
plastic and holds it in place – so, no glue, screws,
nuts, bolts or nails!'

out of this studio. It started as a one-off studio piece that was very difficult and demanding, one that didn't altogether make sense – and it definitely wouldn't pass any marketing boardroom. It had lots of bad points in terms of marketing. So we never thought people would want to buy it in heavy quantities. But because I did it first as a studio piece, and because it then attracted so much attention, and because it had a rather photogenic image – for all these reasons – the company, Kartell, decided to do it. I'm sure they did it initially for column inches only, for publicity. I don't think they imagined it was going to make money.

Collings

Like you, they didn't see it as commercial?

Arad

They didn't, but then it was exactly that: a commercial hit. It was not only

Right
Large Bookworm
Flexible shelving, 1992
Tempered steel
Edition of 20
One Off

'Big, wild and dangerous – the tempered steel Large Bookworm had no idea it was to become a plastic industrial bestseller.'

Below
Bookworm
Flexible shelving
1993
Extruded PVC
Kartell

Opposite
Sketch of a design for the brackets of the Bookworm shelving.

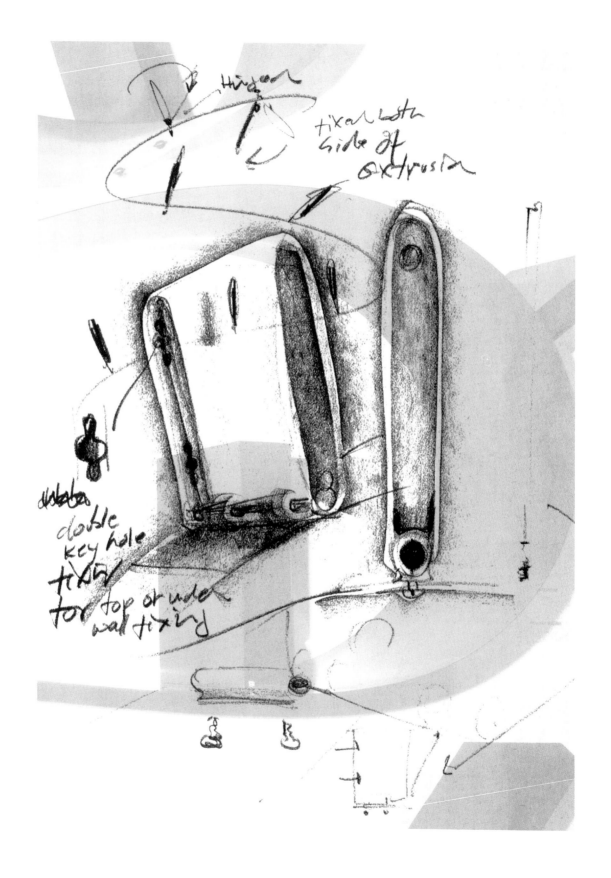

our best selling piece, but it was also their best selling piece for quite a long time. And I think there's this magic number: they extrude over 1,000 kilometres every year. It's a piece I now see everywhere. I mean, if I walk from here to Belsize Park, I know all the windows, and I look through and there it is.

Collings

Bookworms in the front rooms...

Arad

The nice thing is that it's a totally industrial production, against all the odds. So there's an example of something that isn't commissioned but starts life as a studio piece, something that we do without ever thinking about cost of production – which is always the main consideration for an industrial. We ignore it. We do things. A company takes them up. Another example is the Tom Vac Chair. The Tom Vac was born from an installation I did. Domus magazine commissioned a sculpture for the centre of Milan. I proposed to do a realistic sculpture of 100 chairs stacked up on top of each other. I could have taken a ready-made plastic chair, but I used the budget provided to invest in a tool that made vacuum-formed aluminium chairs. This isn't totally industrial because it takes time: it takes twenty minutes to heat the stuff up and suck it into a shape. The shape was originated as a vacuum-formed piece for the Domus project and for a small limited studio run, and then Vitra took the very same shape and made it an injection moulding. So now instead of twenty minutes it takes twenty seconds. That's more industrial. And it's been a very successful exercise.

Collings

So the sequence was that the chair was first considered as part of an art installation, then as a studio piece, and then it was industrially distributed?

Arad

Yes. Another time I did some big, big aluminium bowls that were totally useless and Alessi says, 'Can you make miniatures of them?' Normally, you could have a miniature of something useful and the miniaturizing will render it useless. But here it was the other way round. I made these useless big bowls for which nobody could find a use or a place, and by being miniaturized they became a successful industrial project.

Collings

They became bowls rather than absurd kind of comments on bowls?

Arad

Yes. The same happened to some big aluminium vases I did. These started with a fascination with the process: I found I could blow aluminium, I could make these big shapes and I could polish the stuff so that it becomes reflective. Of course this is to avoid the question of what it is exactly: I mean, is it functional? Is it not? Is it sculpture? I was interested in doing these things and not caring what they're going to be. But then after the bowl had been successful Alessi took these vases too. Then there's all the carbon

Below
Domus Totem
Temporary public sculpture in Milan
1997
Vacuum-formed aluminium shells,
stainless steel

This piece was commissioned by Domus for the Milan furniture fair. 'We said "How about a very realistic sculpture of, say, 100 stacking chairs?".'

Opposite
Tom Vac
Chair
1997
Vacuum-formed aluminium, stainless steel
Edition of 500
Ron Arad Associates

The budget for the Domus Totem was used to make the mould for the aluminium vacuum-formed Tom Vac chair.

Pic Chairs

1997
Polyester and glass fibre, stainless steel
Ron Arad Associates
Edition of 20 unique pieces

'These glass fibre mock-ups for the Tom Vac
were first made as studies, but later, while we
were waiting for the mould to be made and
production to start, we began playing with
pigments and polyester – the result the Pic
Chairs, which in turn were sort of a rehearsal
for the New Orleans series.'

S.O.S.
Shelving system
2003
Extruded polypropelene
Magis

Montage illustrating S.O.S. (Sort of Shelving) that was produced for 'Taking Liberties', an exhibition of Ron's work held at the Centre Santa Monica, Barcelona in 2003.

S.O.S.
Installation of modular shelving system in Milan
2003
Extruded polypropelene
Magis

'S.O.S. is a system we are currently working with
Magis to develop into a commercial product.
The idea is that people will be able to order a
made-to-measure set of shelving elements that
fit a particular space – straight or curved. What
we made to show the shelving at the furniture
fair in Milan was an ambitious folly that very
nearly didn't take off. The installation of the
prototype was intended to be a ball that you
could walk inside, but we didn't quite make it
before the opening, so it turned something a bit
different – but nobody ever knew that!'

fibre pieces. The shapes for these are originated using computers and modelling. But an artisan works on the object. So there's a contradiction there: high tech origination of forms, but then someone working the stuff manually like in the old days. I'm talking about those objects you saw just now in the studio.

Collings

Oh yeah, those chairs.

Arad

They're part of the Paperwork collection. Some have now found themselves going into industrial production, modified and adapted to plastic, which is the main material for mass production. There isn't a better material than plastic.

Collings

When did you start getting into mass production?

Arad

When I was asked.

Collings

What's your attitude towards it now? Is it different, or was there nothing much to change? Has it always been the same?

Arad

When I had to find a company name at the beginning of the 80s, I decided on 'One off' because it reflected my frame of mind at the time. I thought that to design things you have to design something every time – I was ignorant and idiotic about mass production. It's only later I discovered the pleasure and delight of mass production, the beauty of it, which is that you can still design everything like you're designing for the first time, but it's multiplied. But to answer the question of how it works and how I feel about it – let's see. There're all sorts of directions. Sometimes I'll hit on an idea, and it doesn't matter where it comes from, we'll develop it anyway without knowing what company it's for. And then we'll think about it. We'll sit down and discuss: who does it suit, this project? Which would be the best company to do it? And other times there are requests. Alessi asks – can you design the entire collection for a professional barman? You know, the cocktail shaker, the bits, everything. A big chunk of the business is the shaker. This Alessi cocktail shaker I'm holding was designed in the 1950s, and it's very difficult to improve on it. It evolved that way. Think of the angles of a shaker, the two parts – everything about it. It's difficult to do anything else. If you come up with a shaker design that's way out and then it goes through reality checks, well, it'll just go back to what it was in the 50s, which is what it needs to be. Now that's an interesting point from which to start a project. And I believe I found something that's different and better! Whether the barman's union will like it or not, we don't know yet. But Alessi employed a bar consultant and he was thrilled by what we did. The main thing is that the shaker's got to crush the ice, as you're

Chiringuito Ice Bucket
Computer rendering
2004
Stainless steel, glass, plastic
Alessi

Chiringuito Cocktail Shaker
Computer rendering
2004
Stainless steel, glass, plastic
Alessi

shaking it. So this one crushes it on the floor and on the ceiling. The shape is a double-cone, so the ice has a chance to get hit on the way up. I twisted it like a scoop.

Collings

It's got a waist?

Arad

Well, it's just twisted, that means that the ice is hit all the way from top to bottom – that ice hasn't got a chance!

Collings

So this is an example of where a company has given you a challenge and asked if you can do something you might never have thought to do yourself – you know that the 50s shaker really is already ideal enough. But then you have a go and you come up with something. Other times it's different: there's no company in mind, but you come up with something on your own anyway.

Arad

Sometimes I have some loose projects that we didn't yet convince an industrial company to invest a lot of money in. There're about ten companies we work with and they tend to be the better ones in the field. So if it's an upholstery piece of furniture, I know who's the best, and if it's a special sort of plastic, I know who's the best for that, too – whatever. Then there're loads of requests, fresh ones, which we normally don't take unless they provide the opportunity to do a project that could not be done with any of the existing companies we work with – but really we tend not to take them.

Chiringuito Cocktail Range
2004
Stainless steel, glass, plastic
Alessi

'We were commissioned to design a new range
of cocktail equipment for Alessi – which
became the Chiringuito pieces. Although Alessi
already had a flawless cocktail shaker,
professional barmen say there are significant
improvements in ours, particularly the one-
handedness and the twisted form that aids ice
crushing. The ice-bucket houses two bottles and
is designed to be hung on the table to save space
on the top. The range also features a mixing
glass and a man-powered cocktail stick/stirrer.'

Opposite
AYOR
Chair
1991
Patinated steel, lead
Edition of 20
1991–1999 One Off
2000–2004 The Gallery Mourmans

'With the AYOR (At Your Own Risk) chair, the
weighted hollow volume makes the piece tip
forward so it is hardly recognisable as a chair –
it only becomes a chair when you sit on it, and
even then, it feels like it shouldn't support your
weight. But, magically, it does!'

Sit
Chair
1990
Patinated steel and tempered steel
Prototype/edition of 20
One Off/The Gallery Mourmans

'The Sit is part of a collection of furniture that
experiments with tempered steel. This piece
was later developed into an upholstered
product for Moroso's Spring Collection.

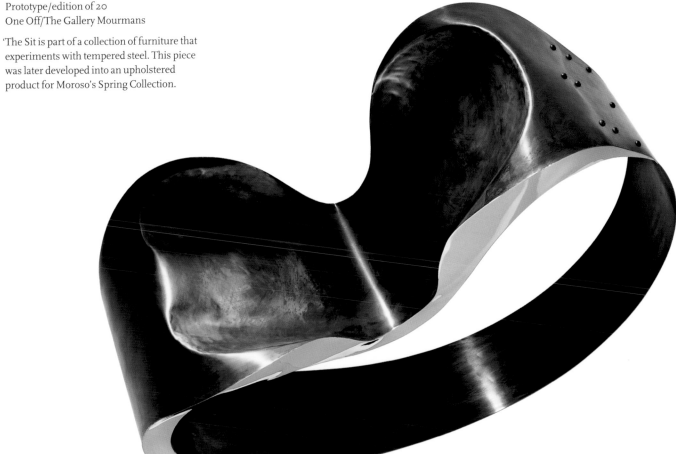

Paperwork Collection Oh Void Daybed

2002
Carbon fibre, Nomex resin-impregnated paper
Edition of 20
The Gallery Mourmans

'The experiment of cloning older pieces like the
Well Tempered Chair, Big Easy and Little Heavy
into carbon fibre versions was followed by the
Paperwork Collection, designed especially to
exploit the properties and characteristics of
lightweight composite structures.'

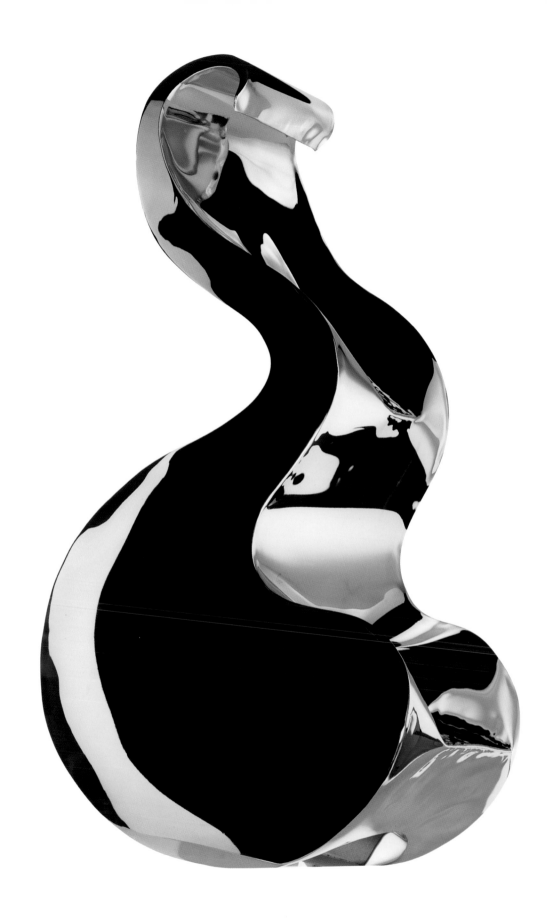

Right
AYOR
Chair
1991
Stainless steel
Edition of 20
One Off/The Gallery Mourmans

Far right
Chair
2003
Blue stainless steel
Edition of 6
The Gallery Mourmans

8
What makes architects tick?
Tel Aviv Opera House, Big Blue and Belgo

What makes architects tick?

Collings

What are your principles of good architecture?

Arad

If it's interesting, exciting, stimulating – if it does good things to you. But is there a recipe? I don't know. Sometimes it's space; sometimes it's surfaces. Sometimes it's both. Sometimes it's a clever mechanical thing, a solution for fixing glass to an opening, or something. But it's a funny occupation because it relies on clients so much, on first of all being asked to do something.

Collings

You mean you're someone's slave right from the beginning?

Arad

Oh yes. It's this élite creative profession where you can express yourself and you can do, you know, whatever. But you have to provide a service for someone who's the final judge of how successful you are at that moment. It's true that good building should still be good long after the person who commissioned it is dead. But in the making of it – in the process of creating it, of making the architecture happen – the client is very instrumental, because first of all he's paying for it. He wants something. He's chosen you to do it. He has his ideas of what he wants, which you either provide him as he's asked for them, or else you explain to him gently why that's not what you want to do. But it's not like when you write a song or paint a painting – you don't do those things with a client in mind in quite that way.

Windwand
Public sculpture
1999
West Ferry Circus, London
Composite materials (predominantly fibreglass and resin), electronics, LEDs
Canary Wharf Riverside

Windwand
Public sculpture
1999
West Ferry Circus, London
Composite materials (predominantly fibreglass
and resin), electronics, LEDs
Canary Wharf Riverside

The Windwand in position at West Ferry Circus,
next to the Thames. This flexible mast was the
winning entry in a competition to design a
public sculpture for the Canary Wharf area.
'Windwand was designed to sway and move in
the wind – it was topped by a bank of LEDs that
responded to multidirectional movement. The
mast's movement and suppleness contrasted
with the static nature of the surrounding real
estate. In the end, the Windwand was built on a
site next to the Thames, where the more open
environment unfortunately weakened the
impact of the piece.'

Collings

Not so directly. But there are still the invisible judges.

Arad

Yeah, the anxiety or the encouragement of wondering what some art critic
like you would say about it!

Collings

You're saying that with architecture the required lift-off power in the first
place is so much greater and the money so much more serious: so the
freedom is exactly less in proportion to all that?

Arad

Really the architecture will only be as good as the client. In a funny way the
client has the bigger role. This is an exaggeration but maybe it's a useful one.

Collings

Architecture was very important for you, when you were young: it was your
springboard. It was what you learned first.

Arad

A safety net rather than a springboard: when I studied architecture it wasn't
at all because I actually wanted to be an architect. As a group, architects
are not the most exciting people. They have lots of different agendas that
sort of take precedence over what started them off. It's an effort to survive,
to make a career, and you have to go through lots of re-thinking.

Collings

The way you put it, it sounds as though there's inevitably a kind of creative
corruption that sets in.

Arad

Like every profession, yes, only with architecture it's more obvious,
because of the dependence on commissions. Of course back then there
was an idea of architecture as something that was free of clients – the
Archigram period.

Collings

But those guys still couldn't have made buildings from their radical
drawings and radical ideas unless a client wanted the buildings done.

Arad

They just made the drawings, yes. There was that American artist,
Vito Acconci...

Collings

Yeah, he did something that came originally from art – from the
Performance Art and Body Art of the late 60s – and a bit from poetry, too,
and then since the 80s he went more and more into architectural ideas.

Arad

That's right, and nowadays he's discovering the thrill that you can get from
commissions. It's a funny thing, the way he speaks – he repeats everything.
I always assumed it was an impediment. I thought, 'Ah, that's why he's a
poet, that's why he's a poet.'

Windwand

Public sculpture
1999
West Ferry Circus, London
Composite materials (predominantly fibreglass
and resin), electronics, LEDs
Canary Wharf Riverside

'The Windwand was made in one 56-metre-long
mould by marine engineers who specialise in
building masts. Their conventional brief was
reversed here – normally engineers are asked to
ensure a mast offers maximum rigidity, whereas
our mast had to be able to sway in the wind.'

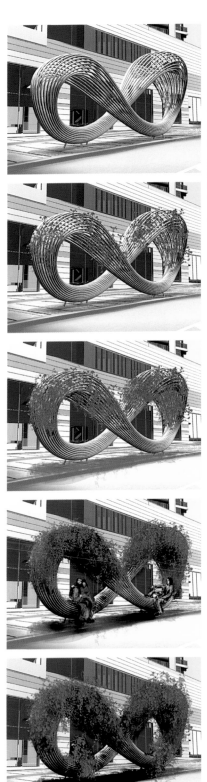

Evergreen!
Public sculpture
2003
Roppongi Hills, Tokyo
Bronze, earth, ivy

Mori

'This piece was commissioned to form part of
the public art provision for a mixed-use building
development by Mori in the Roppongi Hills.
The worst thing about public art is that it is
relatively easy to install, but almost impossible
to get rid of. I wanted this piece to incorporate
its disappearance by eventually being
completely covered by the ivy.'

Tel Aviv Opera House, Big Blue and Belgo

Collings

What was the first bit of real architecture you did? I mean, when you were really yourself, as opposed to that short period when you were employed by a firm of architects in the early 70s?

Arad

Our studios. When we did them we were our own client. But my first architectural project for a client in the conventional sense was the work we did for the Tel Aviv Opera House, finished in 1994. It took four years. I felt a bit like a con man. I didn't know how to do those things. No one did: they'd never been done before. And in any case, I hadn't done a building before. My reputation came from design not architecture.

Collings

Did you think, 'Well, I can do it. I can always do everything.'

Arad

Yes. I'm an optimist.

Collings

But four years is a long time, isn't it?

Arad

Yes. I resigned in the middle because I didn't get on with the other architect, although he was a great man. It was really his building that I did my spaces in. And then there was the Big Blue in Canary Wharf. It doesn't have an entrance or a fire escape or any of those things architects are such experts in. It's that big ten-ton disc there, in Canada Square – I did it in 2000. And then of course there was the Amiga House, which I designed but which failed to get planning permission. That was a house with no door, no windows and no roof. But as I say, it was blocked. I did the Canary Wharf right after the planning application fell through, because I thought now I'd taught myself everything there was to know about composite structures.

Collings

So the sequence of architectural projects was a space within the Tel Aviv Opera House in the early 90s, then nothing, because the next project was blocked, and then the Big Blue in 2000: an interior space, a blocked house and a kind of public, non-functional object, kind of an art object?

Arad

Yes. And there were also some shop designs and restaurant designs. For example the Belgo restaurant in Chalk Farm just near our studio – I did a lot of work on the annex of that place. That was 1994. The issue with all these things was why should anyone give anyone a job if they haven't done anything in that area before? The rules were that you first had to work for another architect for ten years. You had to accumulate bad habits – or

Ron Arad Studios
1989
Chalk Farm, London

'Landscaping the floor in the front part of what was the showroom was a demarcation device, an alternative to using partition walls. This image also shows the calligraphic structural columns and the PVC windows.'

Foyer elements in the Tel Aviv Performing Arts Centre

1994
Tel Aviv
City of Tel Aviv

'This project was made up of a series of autonomous structures/buildings that each performed a different function in foyer space of the arts centre. They created a unique spatial relationship amongst themselves, and with the main building.' Below: a window detail. Bottom: the box office component of the scheme. Below right: a plan of illustrating how the foyer elements fit into the overall building.

what's called 'experience'. Otherwise how will you get anyone's trust? You know Frank Gehry was a late-starter as an architect, too. He told me he was a very successful furniture designer before that. He had to stop doing furniture in order to be taken seriously as an architect. In my case, I don't know – I was never a fully paid-up member of the profession, anyway. I always kept up the other things. Which was ingrained from the first, you know, when I was deliberately making myself an outsider at the AA.

Collings

How did you get the Amiga House commission?

Arad

The clients had seen the Tel Aviv Opera House. They thought whoever designed that can do our home. It was a place in Hampstead, near Kenwood House. And I had this idea of a design with no doors or windows, as I said.

Collings

And there are some pretty nice modernist buildings in that area?

Arad

Well, no, actually, they're sort of crass, pastiche, vulgar red brick...

Collings

But in Hampstead on the whole there are some great buildings, from all periods...

Arad

On the whole, yes, but in this particular road, no – in any case, at first English Heritage supported us big time. They put my plan on the cover of

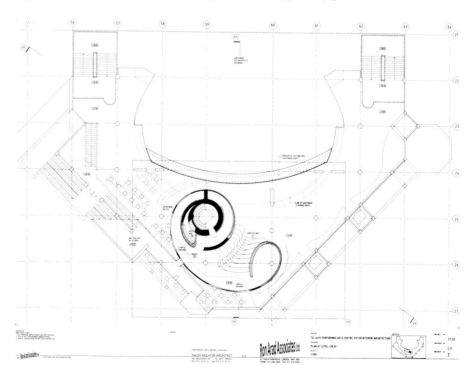

Ron Arad Studios
1989
Chalk Farm, London

'One undulating, translucent PVC roof over steel ribs and structural steel mesh, hovering above what was initially a showroom, a design office and a workshop. It was an interesting and affordable way of transforming the old shed we had bought – to bring light into a restricted space and unify a split-level site.'

Previous
Big Blue
Sculptural/architectural skylight
1999
Canada Square, Canary Wharf, London
Canary Wharf

'Big Blue forms a skylight over the shopping
mall in Canada Square. The highly-reflective,
hollow composite structure was brought to the
site in one piece and placed on top of a glass
cylinder, allowing light into the underground
space and also acting as a distorting periscope
that reflects the outside world.'

Below
Amiga House
Unrealised project
1997
Kenwood, London
Amiga family

Bottom
Computer-rendered photomontage of Daniel
Libeskind's design for an extension to the
Victoria & Albert Museum, London – a project
dubbed 'The Spiral'.

their annual report, and they said this was exactly the kind of house they'd like to see in a conservation area, because it was sympathetic to the woodlands there. And I thought it was all going to work and it was going to go ahead. Because, as you say, Hampstead has traditionally been the home for a lot of creative modern people: for example, Goldfinger's house, Lubetkin's Highpoint, John Winter's Cor-Ten steel house, Michael Hopkins' Hightech, Richard Rogers in Pond Street and others. But the Amiga House proposal was attacked a lot by a local resident, the son of the architect who designed Centre Point, funnily enough. And it was blocked in the end by the person who was in charge of planning for the borough, Nicky Gavron, this great liberal from the past who got Jackson's Lane Community Centre off the ground. What she said at the hearing was that it pained her to turn down good, or very good, architecture but – and this was her phrase – 'We are here to protect not only the very good and the excellent but also the good enough'. So although I can't see how she was really doing it exactly, I can see that she thought she was doing the right thing. The 'good enough' was the insignificant, dilapidated, Golders Green type of house, of which there are millions.

Collings

And you wanted to knock one of those down in order to make your house without any windows or roof?

Arad

Yes. At least, the client who had enough money for the plot would have knocked the original place down: it was a sort of a stylistic mishmash, nothing to write home about.

Collings

So what do you feel the big story here? What was the real point of resistance to your design?

Arad

It's a very conservative community there.

Collings

So it's conservatism? Philistinism?

Arad

Yes. But I don't know if that's the bigger picture exactly, because in the same week the Spiral at the V&A got planning permission: the Daniel Libeskind extension. And that's definitely a radical bit of architecture, especially when you consider the area – South Kensington. It's really quite amazing that it got planning permission. We thought it was a new time: you know, the new Blair government, Cool Britannia. We thought it was going to be the friend of progress. A couple of weeks before this, I'd been invited by No. 10 to join the creative industry. This minister, Mark Fisher – he wrote that book with Richard Rogers about London – well he asks, 'Ron, how can you help us help you?' And I say, 'It's very simple. Abolish planning regulations. The world would be a better place.' I don't think

Belgo Noord and Belgo Centraal
Restaurant interiors
1994 and 1995
Chalk Farm (Noord) and Covent Garden
(Centraal), London
Belgo

'The trick in the design of these two restaurants was to make the restaurateurs believe that the project had as much to do with their Belgian themepark as it had to do with our architectural agenda – the results were surprising, but ones we all enjoyed.'

there should be special cases. The government shouldn't protect the community from us architects, and then say, 'Ah, yes, but you are good architects. What about bad architects?'

Collings

So you think the bad architecture problem would be self-solving? It would be weeded out by people's natural enthusiasm or distaste for badness?

Arad

The whole city is covered by billboards anyway.

Collings

Ugliness is going to exist anyway?

Arad

Yes. Ugliness. Creepiness. But I mean – really, what exactly are they protecting people from with these regulations? Sure, we might get a few bad buildings but don't we get them anyway? The best example is Courtney Avenue. Unfortunately you can't see it, because the guard won't let you.

Collings

Because it's a gated community?

Arad

Yeah, so really, who are they protecting? Every house there has a huge wall, and five four-wheel drive cars and a Mercedes and a sports car. It's ridiculous. It has nothing to do with the Kenwood atmosphere, except it's all done in this fake upper-class style – Hansel and Gretel would be embarrassed to live there.

Collings

Well as you say it's a paradox, since the Libeskind spiral in the context of those old beautiful buildings in South Kensington is a much more radical change to the environment. It's a very established area where things don't change. What would you say was the main new thing about your Amiga House design?

Arad

The fact that the 'shell', as it's called, was literally a shell. I always describe it with my two hands, like doing two shells together. One is stronger than the other and there are gaps. I don't know how to put it – it just holds space. Once the cladding is up, of course, there're no openings or gaps.

Maserati showroom

2003
Modena, Italy
Maserati

Below: The strip of images was Ron's entry for a
book published by Olympus Cameras in 2003.
Most of the other entries were by photographers.
'With my 10 pages, I tried to demonstrate how
design work starts with two dimensions –
first rough sketches, then studied drawings,
computer modelling and rendering – then,
through construction, moves into a three-
dimensional space and becomes an object. This
is the reverse route taken by photography, where
the three-dimensional space/object is squeezed
into the two-dimensional.' Opposite: a sketch
for the design of the showroom's sample wall,
which showcases options for combinations of
finishing and upholstery.

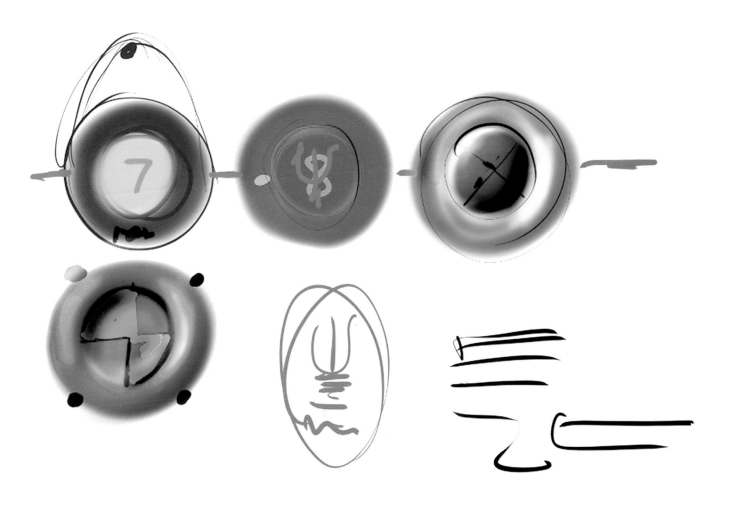

Maserati showroom

2003
Modena, Italy
Maserati

Computer renderings and photographs of the
showroom showing the giant loop that serves as
the stage for displaying cars, and the sample
wall and seating whose design echoes this
looping, curving motif in miniature.

The Qatar floor project

Collings

Do you think of the work you did for the Sheikh of Qatar as architecture or design?

Arad

Architecture. We showed it in the Architecture Biennale in Venice in 2003. Some people thought it was the best thing there – we still get emails all the time about it.

Collings

It was a very grand model for a very grand, mad, sort of science fiction environment – a space with a floor that literally undulates. You have some controls, and you can make the floor ripple. Is the Sheikh of Qatar ever going to have it made?

Arad

Oh yes, within the next two years. But in the meantime we have the contract to develop it. And we're doing a lot of other pieces for him. He has a programme. He's always commissioning things – not just from me.

Collings

How does he see you, what does he think you are?

Arad

He's a fan. It's an interesting relationship. Maybe he doesn't see me enough as a regular architect, because he's commissioned a lot of things from other people that actually we could have done! But he didn't occur to him because we seemed special.

Collings

Is this a problem that he realizes he has?

Arad

No, it's a problem I have!

Collings

You think he pigeonholes you in a way that's limiting: the 'mad creative

Interior elements for the Millennium House

2001–
Doha, Qatar
Sheikh Saud al Thani

This project comprises two interior elements for the Millennium House, an extensive villa complex that is currently being built by a Qatari sheikh for his family. 'We were asked to do the reception room and family dining room. It is a very rare case of a project with hardly any limitations: not of budget, culture or planning – so, a great opportunity to implement new ideas. In the larger reception room, there is a programmable floor that can support constant or frozen movement, can be landscaped, has memory and can create furniture at will.'

Interior elements for the Millennium House

2001–
Doha, Qatar
Sheikh Saud al Thani

A study of the one of the 600 actuators that together form the pixel-style floor of the reception room for the Millennium House. 'Initially, the actuators were conceived as having a mechanical screw movement that would have produced intolerable noise – later, hydraulic and pneumatic options were considered, but the floor will now finally employ totally silent magnetic lifts.'

genius?

Arad

Yes. So when he wants a concert hall for his country...

Collings

He gets a paid-up architect.

Arad

Yeah! And we could do a better job for sure. So I have to sort of bring it home to him. Actually that's what I did recently.

Collings

Did he get the message?

Arad

Yes. He started with me about who could build an exhibition/theatre for 1,000 people...who do I recommend? And I said to him, 'No one could do it better than us.' And he was like, 'Oh, OK'.

Collings

How do you divide things up at the studio – architecture upstairs, design downstairs?

Arad

Well, yes, more or less. But mentally I like to think it's more a continuum. For architects though, it suits them to have me on the outside and not on the inside. They're quite happy for me to be a designer and not an architect. It makes their life easier. Just like it makes artists feel better to not even consider what one does as something that might touch them. And in a funny way it also makes hardcore designers feel a bit better to dub me as an artist. You know, 'Ah, yeah the arty designer.' In reality I can do practical things or I can do hardcore industrial stuff like nobody's business.

Collings

Well, it's understandable apart from professional rivalry, as well, of course. I mean, it's an effort for people to accept that somebody can be good at more than one thing. What brief did the Sheikh give you?

Arad

It was to do a reception space for the Sheikh's palace.

Collings

Some established artists were also invited to contribute ideas for the palace, weren't they?

Arad

David Hockney did a swimming pool. Richard Serra did a sculpture, Ettore Sottsass did another reception space.

Collings

What exactly was the undulating floor thing you did? How did you come up with it?

Arad

Well, I think it came out the way it did because in the first place there was no real need for anything there, because he has other reception rooms.

Here was a project that had no limits. And in architecture you're used to limits as, in a way, the first marks on the canvas. You know: there's a tree here, there's a cliff here, there's a spire over there. And then the client wants this and he wants that. But here there was none of that. Not even a budget limit – and usually of course that's the main limit of all, the one that really decides everything. Plus there wasn't even the client's wife to interfere, or the client's husband, or whatever. And there was no planning permission problem, because this guy is the Minister of Culture!

Collings

And he hadn't asked for anything in particular just a reception space for the villa?

Arad

Only that it has to be next to the dining space of the villa. So I said, 'What do you think of the floor?' I thought you can change the whole space by changing the floor. You can turn it into an amphitheatre and then you can

A sketch plan of the dining room area, a space defined by amphitheatre-style banquette seating.

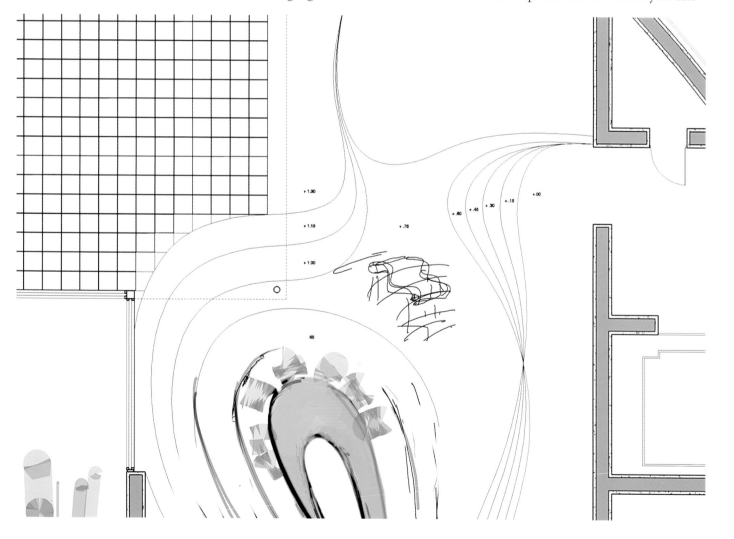

Interior elements for the Millennium House

2001–
Doha, Qatar
Sheikh Saud al Thani

A computer rendering of the reception room in
the Millennium House. 'The balls act as seating
– because they're made from memory foam,
they will always spring back to shape. The idea
is that they are scattered in the room and move
at will around the changing landscape.'

Interior elements for the Millennium House

2001–
Doha, Qatar
Sheikh Saud al Thani

Left: Another view of the dining room area.
'Because the block made up of the seating
pit and table isn't totally enclosed by the space,
it can be seen in the form of an architectural section.'

Right: The lights in the reception room move like
planets on a track that outlines a growing spiral.
Made from advanced silicon and lit by a stick-
mounted LEDs, these orbs can be placed, expanded
or retracted, and coloured by remote control.

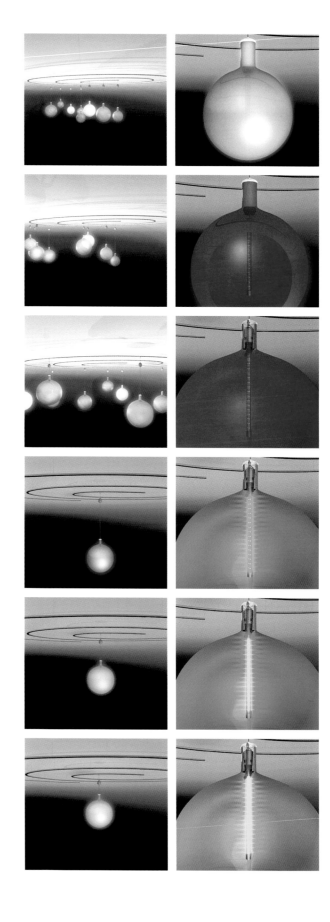

change it back again. Or you can lift something – you can lift the floor in a certain area, and so lift the position of a sofa, say. The floor is a three-dimensional pixel board on to which you can type anything you want. Like Barbara Kruger's LED signs…

Collings

Jenny Holzer's?

Arad

Yeah, sorry, her! But this is a three-dimensional version. And it doesn't light up. It moves. It goes up and down. So you can make like a low resolution auditorium.

Collings

There are these little geometric units, which go up and down.

Arad

Yes, according to a computerized control. The Sheikh holds the control in his hand. He can say, 'I want to have the room exactly as it was a year ago'

– or as it was a week ago. Or, 'I'll have a watery effect.' Then he moves his finger and there's the effect. Or he can do furniture. He'll have a sofa. A three-seater? OK! Put in three-seater. And if he wants, he can drag the form, move it. So the funny thing is, although the sofa is real, and you can sit on it, the movement is virtual, because it's like a message on a pixel board. The shapes of the floor move, say, from one side of the room to the other – it's a sofa-shape, say. But it's not the same sofa it was.

Collings

So the little cubes, which you call pixels, are in an arrangement – they make a sofa on the other side of the room, which is made up of different cubes than were making the sofa on the opposite side of the room earlier. But when you drag it, using the controls, the feeling is that it's the same sofa going across the room, like an animated movie.

Arad

Yes exactly.

Collings

So you provided him with something a little bit like people's recent fantasy of The Matrix.

Arad

Yes.

Collings

He can change his environment by pressing a switch.

Arad

Yes. It is a matrix. That's exactly what it is. And just to add some fun, I included some balls on it that will roll according to the changing landscape.

Collings

Big spheres?

Arad

Big spheres.

Collings

Made out of what?

Arad

Out of Tempur memory foam.

Collings

They roll on the undulating floor without hurting anybody?

Arad

Without hurting anyone. And also there are the light balloons. They move too. Each can be anywhere it wants to be in space, any colour, any size. The Sheikh can change everything with a hand-held remote control: the space, the atmosphere, the size of the room.

Collings

Thinking back to the location of your cancelled Amiga House, it's as if now you're doing a modern Kenwood House: anyone can go to Kenwood house and enjoy it, it's a fantastic building and it used to be the private property of

Interior elements for the Millennium House

2001–
Doha, Qatar
Sheikh Saud al Thani

A study of the technology that underpins the movable banquette seating in the dining room area of the Millennium House. 'This device allows sitters to move and fidget – each section will allow multi-directional movement: backwards, forwards and sideways.'

someone rich who had it all to himself, because that's the way society was. But now everyone has access. And likewise your Sheikh has invited you to make a fantasy building for him, which in the future anyone will be able to enjoy, because he's going to make it public.

Arad

Like Hampton Court, where anyone can go and see the tennis court.

Collings

Yes, people can enjoy this nutty stuff you're proposing: undulating, science-fiction rooms, with changing sofas, all done with TV remote controls.

Arad

Science-fiction...nutty...yes, that's how he sort of sees himself. And yes he's the nearest thing you might get today to a patron centuries ago.

Collings

It's funny that you've succeeded in scaling the giddy heights but have trouble down at the ground level – you know, trying to get a house going on your own turf, in North London.

Arad

I really wanted the Amiga House to go to Qatar, but in fact although I will be doing a house for him eventually it won't be that one.

Collings

So you're still waiting to burst through as an architect?

Arad

No, I work with six architects in my studio now, and actually we do lots of what is classified as architecture.

Yamamoto

Collings

What are you working on with your architects now?

Arad

I'm doing something for Yohji Yamamoto in Tokyo. He's got some huge space there that he needs to turn into his flagship showroom for his 'Y's' brand. He sent these pigeons to Europe to scout for architects. He sent them to Norman Foster, us and some French people. And then after two weeks of silence he said, 'OK, we decided to use you.' So the other day we sent them our scheme, and we got an email saying how thrilled and excited they were.

Collings

What's your scheme?

Arad

Everything turns slowly, everything changes: there are four huge turntables flush with the floor. They're not synchronized. Meanwhile people are walking around in there, doing their shopping, and they're

Y's Store
Clothing store
2003
Tokyo
Yohji Yamamoto

Below: 'A flagship store in the brand new Roppongi Hills area, in which new shopping streets full of the big-name fashion shops seem to spring up almost overnight.' Opposite: a preliminary sketch exploring the idea of rotating mounts designed to allow the store's display columns to move through 360 degrees. This rotation complements and extends the movement of the display rings that make up the columns, whose motion enables items of clothing to be presented in ever-altering configurations.

walking on and off this structure without even knowing it, because the movement is so slow. When the shop closes someone pulls a lever and the movement speeds up, the turntables go round a bit like washing machines. And I invented this new kind of glass, a bit like corduroy.

Collings

So it's a public space, big and open, with things moving, and some newly invented materials?

Arad

Yes. It's a showroom. And there're some columns made out of stacked tubes like a slinky, so each can be pulled out and become a hanging rail. So it's adjustable: you could have several of these rails, or have them at different heights, forming different shaped volumes.

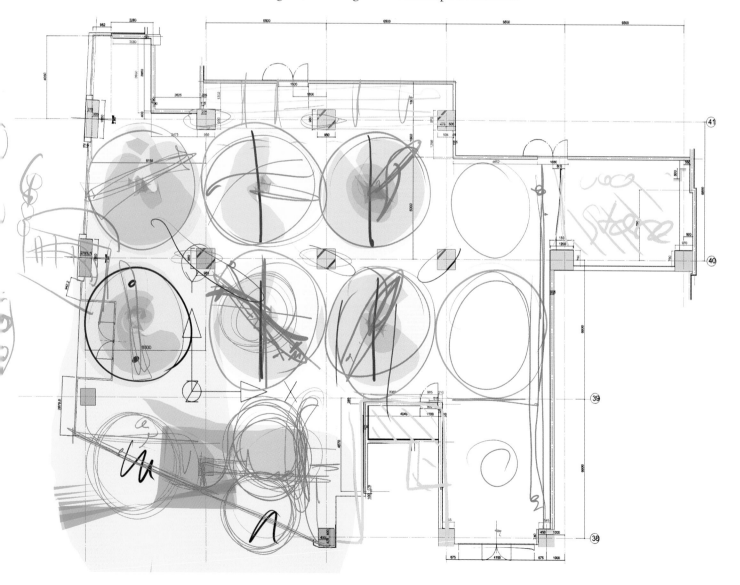

Y's Store
Clothing store
2003
Tokyo
Yohji Yamamoto

Left
'Here, we were inventing shop fittings.
In the stacks of lozenge-shaped rings,
each element can rotate individually
to provide a hanging rail – and where
necessary, shelves – at a particular
height and location.'

Right
'We used a revolving door for the store,
almost as if to power the rotation of
the turntables. The freehand Y and S
that decorate the doors are letters that
appeared in my first sketches and
ended up becoming the store's logo.'

Y's Store
Clothing store
2003
Tokyo
Yohji Yamamoto

Site photos showing elements of the Yamamoto
store, including the glass-tube facade, stacked
epoxy-coated mild steel counter ('very, very big')
and coat-hangers with easy-lift handles.

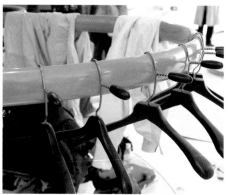

Car park building

Right
Vallarta Tower
Residential development
2003–
Guadalajara, Mexico
JVC Project

'Our proposal tackles one of the main problems of dwellings in a tower block – the parking. As there isn't enough space on the site for surface parking, we have proposed a vertical parking facility to provide the space for two cars per apartment. Underground car parks have not only become notoriously dangerous places, but are also very inconvenient – whereas in this development, a journey to your home doesn't have to include a stop underground and a walk from the car to the lift. Our tower gives you parking at your front door'

Below
Bertrand Golberg
Marina City
1964
Chicago
'An inspiring precedent for a tower that avoids having to have an underground car park.'

Collings

A while ago you showed me a design for a building you were working on, where there was some kind of radical car park. It went up the side of a tall building, and the people could just step out of their flats, on whatever floor they lived, and get into their car, and then press a switch and the lift would glide them down to ground level.

Arad

Well, whatever I do – if someone asks me to design something then I always feel I somehow have to invent it from the beginning. If we go back to the Amiga House, it wasn't that I'd already done a lot of houses and I now did this one in relation to them. It was just from nothing – or from optimism, just thinking and believing that, well, this could work. So when someone asks me to redesign a tower block and redesign the car park as well, I think, well, it's not that I'm subversive. But it's just that I do a bit of calculation about how many floors there are exactly and then I just go into remembering old favourites – I don't know: Goldberg's building in Chicago, Marina Towers, say. A third of that thing is a spiral car park.

Collings

You like the idea that you've got to have the cars, and you think they don't have to be buried underground, they can be out in the open: they can be built into the look of the whole design?

Arad

Yeah, then that sort of leads you into the problem of how to structure the thing, and you now realize it's not a good idea to have cars indoors, so you think, well, let's have two shafts that are sort of outside the building, but completely vertical like the building. Once you've got to that point, that shows you the way the rest of the design must go. Now that's what's good about a competition – that job was a competition in the first place. It wasn't a negotiation with a client. So you just do the competition and win it, and really you're winning this great chance. The place is in Mexico. It was a competition to design a car lot, not a building. But in the event they sold the site before they actually chose the winner! But now they're going to do the project on a new site, so it's all worked out OK.

Collings

In your ideal of what architecture is, is there an element of self-conscious modernity? Or do you think modernity just takes care of itself anyway? I mean, because you're working in the present moment? I suppose I'm asking, are you a Modernist?

Arad

I think newness is important. The way ideas go ahead in any area – in fashion, in art, as well as in architecture – is usually by people joining a bandwagon. But I'm a bit more interested in the actual moment of the

new, in that time where some things, some objects and ideas get born which weren't there before. Maybe that's connected to laziness! I'm not a scholar. I don't have to refer to anything. I don't have to place myself in history, or to carefully align myself with anything. I always think I never really get anywhere by hard, tedious work like that, but simply by having a big idea. The big idea carries everything else along.

Aesthetics, ideas, things changing

Collings

You said you proceeded by having big ideas – tell me more about these.

Arad

They have their sell-by date! In every field: philosophy, mathematics and physics. It's sort of an image: that illusion of knowledge, or the illusion that there is a Solution. It's the same with ideas about politics – communism, whatever.

Collings

When we were young there was an excitement about architecture but at the same time a very strong hatred for modern architecture, wasn't there? It stood for brutality and anonymity. In the last few years it's come to stand for a great feeling of London: you go over the Thames now and you think, 'This is great! Where did we get all this modern architecture!?'

Arad

Ah, and then the horrible buildings are rediscovered.

Collings

They're rediscovered as wonderful buildings: those previously horrible 1970s buildings.

Arad

I remember thinking how ugly 1950s cars were when I was young, with their unnecessary fins and the excessive chrome. Of course like anyone else, I love that look now. It's audacious and optimistic. But back then the same look was ugly and crass. So ideas can change.

Collings

Something from the past becoming attractive, is not merely nostalgia. There's that but there's an open-mindedness about design too now, a willingness to see beauty in a range of things that come from different times. And that open-mindedness is probably peculiar to the last twenty years or so.

Arad

Yes. However I'm not completely open-minded! I know my favourite car is, without any competition, the Citroën DS. That car was so new when it was new, so unlike anything else. And that newness still holds. It's still

Flaminio Bertoni
Citroën DS
1955
Citroën

visible. You don't have to remember it. You see it.

Collings

Do you have an ideal building that is the equivalent of the DS?

Arad

Oh yeah – even the cliché building, Corbusier's Ronchamp. You know it's amazing but then you see it and it's still absolutely breathtaking. I love the taking of liberties you see with that building, just like with the Citroën.

Collings

I wonder if the difference now is that there is a freedom to do what you like, whereas we assume that things in the past had a force of functionalism upon them. We assume they had to obey some kind of law, whereas now there's an acceptance – with Frank Gehry, for example – that the building will be a hyper-building or a meta-building: a comment on the notion of 'a building'. He's given the licence; he's got the job to do nutty buildings. They only refer to themselves. Or they refer to him.

Arad

They're not nutty any more, of course. After him, architects now almost have to apologize for building straight walls. He became the norm so fast. And at that stage you start looking at them not because they are exaggeratedly 'shapey', but you start to actually look at the shapes.

Collings

Yes, although the reason people commission them is for the shapiness.

HotelGrandSalone
Design for a hotel room
2002
Cosmit, Milan

This conceptual design was commissioned by Cosmit, the organisers of the Salone del Mobile furniture fair in Milan in 2002. Ten architects were allotted a different world city to inspire a scheme for 'a hotel room of the future'. The pictured sketch illustrates how Ron's design answers the spatial restrictions of the brief by focusing on a small 'pill box' comprising a circular bed and an omni-directional, interactive bank of screens that hosts a range of audio-visual media, including internet and video messaging. 'What would please me most in a hotel is not someone else's idea of chic, elegance of style, but rather comfort, clarity and ease of access to information, entertainment and ambience.'

HotelGrandSalone
Design for a hotel room
2002
Cosmit, Milan

Right: A detailed computer rendering of the
'pill box' in HotelGrandSalone, illustrating the
ways in which different media – for example,
a football match, a display of local television
channels or atmospheric footage of locations in
the city outside (Ron was allotted Mexico City) –
can totally cocoon the viewer.

Opposite, below: 'The owner of the Hotel Puerto
America – currently being built in Madrid – saw
the exhibition at the furniture fair and asked a
number of the participants, including Ron, to
incorporate elements of their schemes into
designs for different sets of rooms in his new
development. 'Many of the original ideas from
HotelGrandSalone survived the reality check,
including the circular bed and the semi-circular
projection screens. A section of the ring of
screens actually forms the window of each
room, so people outside the hotel can watch
reversed images of TV and films as they pass by.'

Opposite, above: 'The rooms of the Hotel Puerto
America are lozenge-shaped envelopes, and to
save space, all of their functions are incorporated
into a curvaceous monolithic block.'

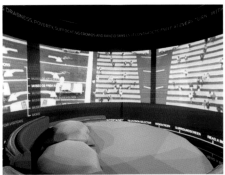

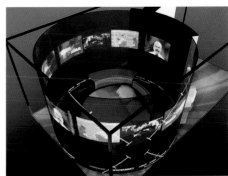

They don't care about what the actual shapes are. At the moment they're being commissioned because of Gehry. He's the name we must have. The commissioning guys don't stroke their chins thoughtfully, or narrow their eyes and tip their heads to one side and say, 'Hmm, I wonder if that curve is quite right with those other curves…'

Arad

No. Because there's something stronger than the actual shape, which is the idea of the shape.

Collings

In the future we'll all maybe see that some Gehrys are better than others. Some periods of him are better. I read something very critical of him by Hal Foster the other day. He saw him as a symptom of spectacularization gone mad.

Arad

Well, Gehry gets away with something that we thought was a no-no. We thought the building is not a sculpture.

Collings

It's got to have some integrity as a building.

Arad

Yeah. And Gehry did get away with it.

Battersea Power Station

Collings

What else are you working on?

Arad

The biggest thing is the Battersea Power Station. I mean, if you were a journalist I wouldn't be able to talk to you, because it's too soon to declare it. But as this is a book and books take time to produce I think we can take the chance.

Collings

Who's the client?

Arad

A development company from Hong Kong, called Parkview. They want to do good things for London. One of them is to give back the Power Station to the people. But before that, it's got to go through the hands of all sorts of people: architects, consultants, copywriters, advertisers, image-makers, and…us. Anyway, there's some leaflet that was produced by a company called Future Brands. They came up with images for London. And guess what, they were? Sarah Lucas with eggs on her breasts, and Jamie Oliver with 'thank you' on his forehead – this is their idea of London. Actually, for me it's kind of 'off'. We've moved on a bit since ten years ago, however long it is since that stuff was hot! When New Labour came into power, they tried to do this Cool Britannia thing: the same kind of thing that this publicity

Hotel complex in the roof space of Battersea Power Station

2003
London
Parkview Development

An early computer-rendered version of the view looking from the north to the south hub of the hotel complex. The south hub will comprise a viewing platform, restaurant and bar which – unlike at the VIP north end of the project – will all be open to the public. The two tunnels are horizontal lifts. 'This image also shows what was nicknamed the Lilypad – the floating floor space between the hubs – that was later edited out.'

company is doing. New Labour came up with the Dome – and look what happened there. So now when I see the ideas of Future Brands, I see the Dome before my eyes, like a warning sign. But in any case, they came up with this slogan: 'Involve, imagine, inspire'. Then: 'Why not?' And then on the T-shirt they came up with something else. It doesn't say 'Battersea'. It says 'London': 'London, the Power Station'. Things like that, get me really irritated!

Collings

Because it takes away the flavour that made Battersea, or London, or whatever inspiring in the first place?

Arad

Yeah. It's conning themselves, conning the client, conning everyone. It's not even stating the obvious, but – I don't know – I see it as sort of stating the perceived obvious.

Collings

What will the Power Station be? A theme park, a museum, an environment, a fun fair?

Hotel complex in the roof space of Battersea
Power Station
2003
London
Parkview Development

A sketch exploring an arrival point to the hotel.
'Guests will be "beamed up" from beneath
ground level to the reception area, then taken in
horizontal lifts to their rooms.'

Arad

Well let's see. We know at the end of the day, it's the retail that pays the rent, and the rest is something else, entertainment. I see it as a fantastic venue for things for which we presently don't have good venues in London. Take the Art Fair.

It goes to the horrible, nasty Business Design Centre in Islington. That's the last place you want to do an art fair. So here you've got this place, the Battersea Power Station, which was designed by the same guy who originally designed the building that is now Tate Modern – Gilbert Scott – and who designed the red telephone box, also. Battersea Power Station is an amazing building, and there's this amazing space between the two turbine halls. And London doesn't have a lot of better landmarks. So this could be a fantastic venue for the Art Fair, for London Fashion Week, or London Film Festival – all sorts of things. It's got a space that could contain all of that.

Collings

So when you're concerned about what they're saying to you, the Future Brands people, you're making a statement about your attitude towards architecture. Which is that you're interested in what something already has, in preserving that and not destroying it by fake up-to-date-ness?

Arad

Yes, that's a good way of putting it. You know, when the Tate looked for a new home I was disappointed they went for a conversion and not for a wholly new place. Not that it worked out so bad.

Hotel complex in the roof space of Battersea Power Station

2003
London
Parkview Development

A recent concept sketch articulating the curvaceous forms of the hub elements.

**Hotel complex in the roof space of Battersea
Power Station**

2003
London
Parkview Development

An early illustration showing the rhythm of the
strips of rooms – the doors of which connect
directly with the lift shafts – the arrival point, the
reception – in what's now become the north hub.

Collings

Well, the look of Tate Modern from the outside is nice, yes, and the big entrance. Everything else inside is like any old predictable, populist art centre.

Arad

Look, the place works and we can't argue.

Collings

I find it a trivial place but, sure, it's a big success in terms of ratings, yeah.

Arad

And the Dome definitely wasn't, and at the time you couldn't help comparing the two. So, yes, if you're dealing with Battersea Power Station, it's something that had its own life in the past, and now it's going to be converted, and conversions have their charm. It's a building that's part of a tradition. There's something to dream about there: the brown bricks, the tall chimneys. And when you go there there's a long, long, 170m space with dials and letters – letters that spell 'Ealing'. And you can think to yourself there's a handle there and if you pull that handle there'll be no electricity in Ealing!

Collings

Fantastic.

Arad

It's actually more daunting than science fiction. You think, Hmm, what are they going to do here, a Conran restaurant? We were asked to do a bit of

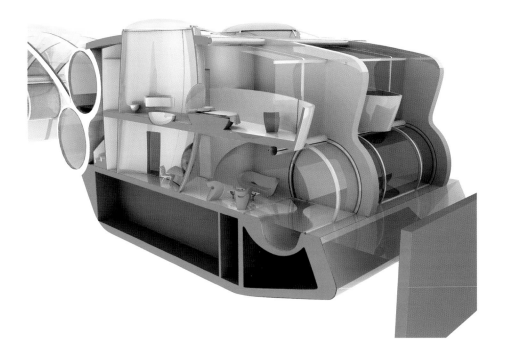

Hotel complex in the roof space of Battersea Power Station

2003
London
Parkview Development

An external view of one of the apartment-style bedrooms. The room's looping structural form creates a split-level space that allows for a public area below (featuring a study/guest bedroom, kitchen/pantry and spa), and a private bedroom and balcony above. The curved glass canopy can be retracted to allow guests to use the spa in the open air.

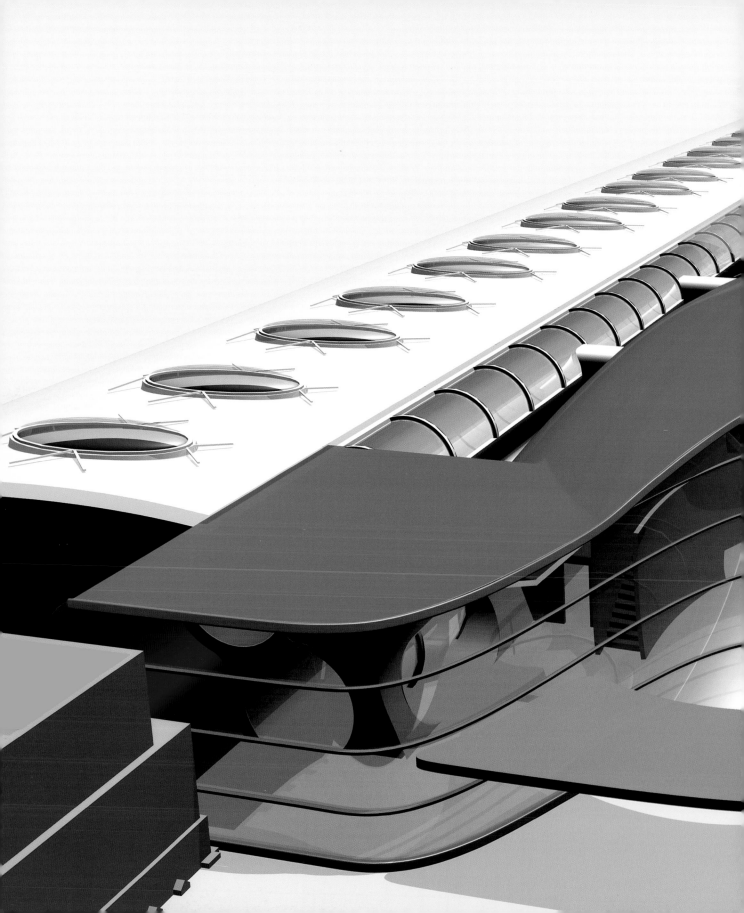

architecture on the roof: actually a hotel that will also be the roof of Battersea Power Station. So that's the answer to your question. What it will be – this is the commission – is a 50-room, £2,000-a-night hotel. The problems are: What can you do in there? How are you going to deal with it? Are you sure there are enough people to pay for it? They said, 'Oh you'd be surprised'! Anyway, there's the building, the brief and there're all sorts of soundbites for all the consultants, copywriters, advertisers, corporate image people, and the graphics people, and so on. There's a lot of talk about the Design Council and about the creative industry. Personally, I'm always very suspicious about the 'sponsored' creative industries.

Collings

What are they?

Arad

I don't know.

Collings

The art world? The film world? The advertising world?

Arad

I think the art world, maybe, isn't an industry. Maybe that's the only world left out! It's the list they made of people that were invited to No. 10 shortly after Blair was elected: fashion people, graphics people, design people, architects. And there was a separate night for all the rock 'n' roll people. For me it looks like the lazy smugness of London.

Collings

Aren't big-money architectural projects always involved or mired in that problem of lazy smugness? Because particularity and specific, creative, good, original art ideas – it's hard to find those things in the context of enormous money.

Arad

It's hard for the authorities to find them, yes. Anyway, these developers are Hong Kong guys, and their programme of development for the Battersea Power Station is going on as we talk now. The head of the developers is in London, and he meets new people here all the time, and each time something new excites him. This week it's us. Then another time he met Cecil Balmond, the engineer that did the Toyo Ito Pavilion that was outside the Serpentine – so now that little pavilion has been bought by the Battersea Power Station. So, back to our concept for the hotel: we said there's a long building here, and there should be some structures that bridge the roof.

Collings

These are your ideas, or this is what you have to deal with – the set-up that's already there?

Arad

It's the same thing: what one has to deal with and one's ideas are very close to each other! And immediately, the first minute into the project, I thought,

Previous
Hotel complex in the roof space of Battersea Power Station
2003
London
Parkview Development

A later rendering of the main facilities area of the hotel at the north hub. The bulging form of the facilities area is placed off-centre, a compensation for the fact that due to logistical concerns the entire complex does not sit centrally within the rectangular perimeter of the Power Station building. This 'imperfection' is a deliberate celebration of the hotel's context: placing the restaurant, bar and reception off-centre means guests can choose to stand in a position that is exactly equidistant between two of the host building's iconic chimneys – the view is the thing.

Hotel complex in the roof space of Battersea Power Station

2003
London
Parkview Development

An initial concept rendering of the journey down one of the complex's horizontal lift shafts. The repeat lines suggest the potential for space to extend ad infinitum. Through the internal wall of the shaft, views are available down onto the lower levels of the Power Station, while on the external wall, an opaque finish protects the bedrooms from public gaze. This public/private mixture echoes the connection in the overall project design between spaces that are accessible to everyone, and spaces that are accessible only to the few.

as it's so long – as I said, it's 170m – what are you going to do? If you're staying there, are you going to walk all this way to your room? So I thought maybe horizontal lifts would be good. There's like, twenty-five rooms on each side. If you're in Room 25 you swipe your card and then you're in the shuttle, and it stops right in your room. It's sort of science fiction. There's some animation, too. You're an ordinary person down below: you look up and you see all these science fiction glass shafts with rich celebrities in them. The guests will be protected, in this dark, glazed, limousine-type space. You have to put a lot of effort into isolating them, because they're stars – only stars can afford to go to this place. You've got to think about how the stars can meet other stars and be protected while they're doing that. And where can the general public go? And how can they all get something out of each other's presence? All these things have to have an architectural solution that will still stand long after the concept of celebrity is gone! It's like Kenwood House, as we were saying earlier. It was

designed for something else, but it now belongs to us. And anyone can go and look at the Rembrandt there.

Collings

It does sound a bit science fiction. But it's all really happening now is it?

Arad

We did an interim presentation for them, at the end of which Victor Hwang, the developer, said it was all much better that he'd imagined it would be. He said he'd seen too many presentations by too many designers. So we asked if we even had to carry on with the other half of the presentation. Because this was an interim presentation, why can't we stop here? So they said OK, and now we have to take our concept to the planning permission stage.

New stuff for Qatar

Collings

Is there another architectural project you're working on that has a different set of problems to Battersea Power Station?

Arad

A totally different set of problems comes up with the work for Qatar: one project is a movable theatre in a park. When you work for these people everything is urgent: it has to be done for the next festival. They have a date of some state function and they want to decorate it with things, with a new theatre. Because it's all fast and decisive they're ideal patrons.

Collings

It has to happen in a hurry, but on the other hand you can do whatever you want?

Arad

It's hurry, but it's all self-imposed. We know that if it doesn't happen after all, if they don't have a theatre by that time, well, never mind, there's the next festival. It seems that nothing is essential, or crucial, that they can't live without. I think they can live without all the treasures they keep buying, but in any case they keep buying them! I mean, the treasures are dinosaurs and mummified pharaohs and a new sculpture by Richard Serra.

What's best?

Collings

Do you think there's a hierarchy of forms and architecture is at the top?

Arad

Absolutely not.

Collings

Do you think that something else is at the top or you don't think anything is at the top?

Arad

Well, this isn't to answer your question directly, but I think there's a tendency to classify. When there was Destructionism and Ruinism, and so on – and Recycling – I was never a champion of any of that. Friends of the Earth put the Rover Chair on the cover of their magazine because they thought it was recycling. But I'm not a good one for religions, or enforcing a trend or a club or anything. And I think I have that open-mindedness too about the big forms: architecture, design, art and so on – I don't care about the distinctions that much. I remember when 'organic' was a buzzword: 'organic shapes', which I simply didn't understand. And the minute anyone starts getting neurotic about curves I just want to do straight lines.

Collings

The reason I asked is because, as we were saying earlier, London is the big architecture city now. It must be great to be part of that – think of the architect who designed the Gherkin.

Arad

Oh, I still don't think there's a hierarchy, though. The Gherkin – yes, definitely, that's great. It's got power, permanence…

Collings

And amusement. It captures people's attention.

Arad

It does, yes. And I'd like to do that. But there's also pleasure when I walk home from work and I spot five windows through which I can see my bookshelves! My Bookworm – people just go to the shop and buy it. And I wasn't even all that serious when I did it. And I can see Tony Blair sitting on one of my chairs on the front page of *The Times*. And the *Big Brother* house last year was full of my furniture: these sofas – I mean, for some people that achievement would be at the top of any hierarchy. We're in my house now. For lots of people this is the *Big Brother* sofa. Friends of my daughter come here and say, 'Oh wow, cool, you got the *Big Brother* sofa.'

Collings

So vitality and potency reside precisely in not getting too grand?

Arad

Oh grandness is not so bad either! It would be good to design the Albert Hall! I mean, I'm very glad I'm doing Battersea Power Station. That's grand.

10
Why curve?

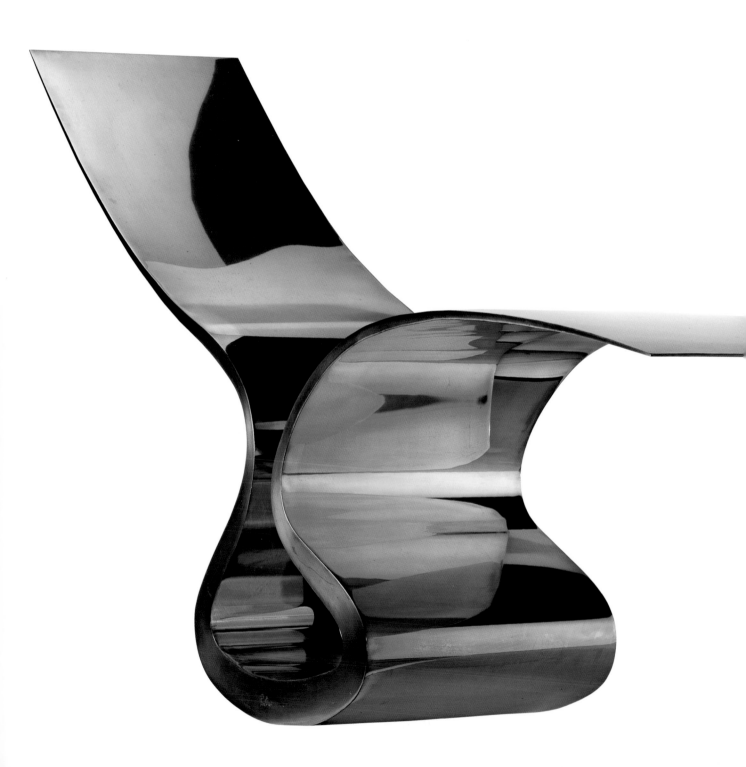

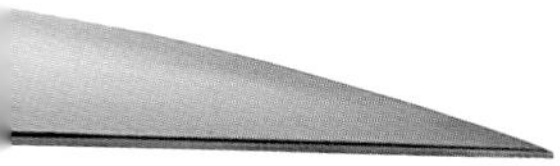

Why curve?

Collings

What about these characteristic curvy lines you do? How do you see them? And in terms of the history of design generally, what do you think they're doing?

Arad

Well, for one thing I don't have any problem with straight lines. Usually curves are more expensive to make. It's a lot easier to produce straight things because they make immediate sense and they're simple. And also, curves in the wrong hands can be terrible. I mean, after Frank Gehry did Bilbao all architects had to do wonky walls. It's the same with people who couldn't resist doing a pediment before, when we had the postmodern craze. So you do see lots of ugliness with curves.

Collings

A straight line is safer?

Arad

Of course – but there's a whole religion around the straight line, as you know...

Collings

There's Modernist Art, abstract paintings with squares, Minimalism...

Arad

Yes, and you've now got Minimalism in design, and architecture – in all sorts of interiors. When we did the Tel Aviv Opera House, before computer technology could assist us, we had to do something like 400 sections where a Minimalist architect would need to do maybe four. Because there wasn't a straight line in any direction.

Collings

So everything slopes and leans?

After Spring
Daybed
1992
Mirror-polished stainless steel, tempered steel
Edition of 5
One Off

'A chair in one line, thickening in the centre and tapering to the extremes. The rocking base appears to be too small to support the rocking movement, but is made stable by the heavy internal weighting. The thin ends contain tempered-steel 'bones' that give them strength and flexibility.'

Arad

Not only that. I mean, the second easiest thing to a straight line is a radiused curve: a curve that you can define by its radius. And there's not a single radius in the Tel Aviv Opera House. It's all done by offsets from a straight line. For example, to do the amphitheatre, the steps were like this, so to define this curve it had lots of lines and dimensions here. The drawings for all that are pretty amazing. And what's more amazing is that they were done, as I say, before we had computers. The office here looked completely different when we were working on that. It was like a sweatshop of drafting. That job was basically four years of sweatshop drafting.

Collings

People making curves?

Arad

They were drawing and writing, and coming up with all these figures. And when we sent a set of drawings to the Italian manufacturer – incidentally, the same people that later ran our Ron Arad studio – the production manager slammed the booklet down on the owner's desk and said, 'Stefano, you see what you can do with computers!' And they went computerized before us because they thought these drawings of ours were computerized. But they were hand-made.

Collings

So that was the peak of curves for you?

Arad

That was the suicide curve – I mean, we were martyrs to it. But we did other things earlier that we didn't believe anyone could build. We'd kind of pretend, you know, 'What's the problem? Hey, it's just two ribs like that'. And we'd make a model out of Lycra, with lots of ribs. Stretched Lycra round ribs and, you know, 'What's the problem?' And in fact when they built it, they used the same technique as we used to make our Lycra model. And they actually cut, profile-cut, all the different ribs. So, yes, we were never scared of curves. When you look at the shelves behind you, where you're sitting now, I mean, they're just a radius and straight lines. It doesn't need to have curves. And there are lots of things like that. The surface of this table we're sitting at is straight. It's just that people shy away from curves.

Collings

The table has a flamboyant, unpredictable contour. It's totally functional of course – it does everything a table must do – but it's got all this curvy action going on as well.

Arad

Yes, the aerial view of it is curved but the surface is level. It's a functioning table. Actually this one comes from a set. You can see them on that poster on the wall over there.

Collings

Where it says 'Ron Arad Studio 38 Tables'?

Arad

Yes, it's part of that big spiral of tables, and that's the plan-view of the room.

Collings

They spiral out from a centre, they go round and round and round, the smaller ones at the centre.

Arad

And we're still selling them. There were thirty-eight of these spirals. We still get orders saying things like, 'Do you have Table No. 9?' Each one was given a number. And we have to say, 'No, sorry'. Because No. 9 would be a small one, near the centre, and those are the ones that always went first.

Collings

Every table is different?

Arad

Every one yes. They're all based on a spine that you can bend. There's some sort of cleverness in the way the legs are attached to the top. And that poster is really still a working document. Someone could look at it and pick out a number and ask, 'Where's that?' And we could get it for them. And if someone wants a long, straight one, they can get it. Or sometimes they want a curve to go a certain way in a room. So there's a choice. And there are some silly ones, that are hardly useful – that are shorter than wide, say. I've seen Table No. 1 in a few houses in Italy.

Collings

It's kidney-shaped, but even that sounds like something relatively standard and well-known. In fact your curves have a very particular feel about them, they seem like they're still being drawn, not as if they've been around for

38 Tables

1995
Mirror-polished stainless steel,
Ron Arad Associates

'A series of 38 tables derived from a freehand
plan that we used to create a maze in an
installation for the 1995 Milan Furniture Fair.
Each section (table) has a unique size and shape.'

ages, not like something classical. What do you think a curve does? Or at least these ones you do – what impression do they make? What need does it answer for people?

Arad

I don't really analyse it. But maybe it's about the freedom to do what you want and not to take orders from rehearsed things that were done before you. Many years ago when I was a student, Arata Isozaki gave a lecture – it's funny, I'm working with him now. He designed the megastructure for the Sheikh of Qatar's villa. Anyway, before computers people used to use French curves. And he said in this lecture, 'Why use these French curves? Why not use the best curves in the world?' And guess what he meant. Of course, this was before political correctness as well as before computers – but he meant the curves of Marilyn Monroe. He actually traced them from photos, and I can show you a Marilyn Monroe chair based on those outlines.

Collings

Were they good curves?

Arad

Sort of, yeah. Very dated, you know: Wonderbra, that kind of thing. But he always did those Marilyn-Monroe-outline curves, using them in different ways – right-way up, upside-down. And as a cheeky student at the time, I asked if I could have one, and he said to write to his office. I don't know if the reason I never got one was because I didn't send the letter after all – or what the reason was. But in any case I never did get one, sadly. I met him ten years later and I mentioned it to him. And then I didn't see him for another ten years or so, when he'd become the chairman of some Japanese award – the Oribei awards. They were named after a Samurai who was a potter as well as a Samurai. He used to let the glazing colours drip, and he sort of preached a doctrine of imperfection. And Isozaki was now the chairman of the judging panel, and that year I got the award. We met in a place near Tokyo and he arrived with a big parcel. It was the Marilyn Monroe curves, which he'd brought for me. But they weren't the same now, they'd been made new – they were more like a special piece now, like Marcel Duchamp's *Trois Standard Stoppages*. Beautiful, really – deep colours, glazed: I'll show it to you next time you come over.

Collings

But all around us, your whole space here is curvy – tables, bookshelves, chairs.

Arad

Well, when I reluctantly started studying architecture, in the first year I declared I'm not going to use tools, ever. Like parallel motions, and set squares and things. It was stupid, but there you are. And it didn't go down very well with my tutor. I thought at that time you could do everything with just a 6B pencil and your eye, or your feel for drawing. So in an act

Left
The original poster for 38 Tables.

Below
Arata Isozaki's stack of perspex stencils outlining the various curves of the body of Marilyn Monroe.

of defiance I said, 'OK – I'll show you tools!' And I bought a whole set of acrylic tools and boiled them so that they weren't regular anymore.

Collings

They became blobs?

Arad

They became, like, not perfect. They were still ruled lines, but the lines weren't straight anymore. But I have to say that as an exhibit they were good. What I was after was not the fruit of the machine but the machine itself. But again, you know, I don't really think about curved lines much. It's just that you're forcing me to analyse them now.

Collings

Yes, I am, because it's the main identifying trademark of what you do. Also, it's the sign of Frank Gehry, I guess. But in the field of design it's really you: wonky curved lines; a flamboyant curve – an exaggerated sign of…what it is it? Being an 'individual'. It seems to be a deliberate attention-grabbing opposite to Minimalism.

Arad

Yes, I suppose you could set up an opposition of a Gehry museum on the one hand: Bilbao Guggenheim. And a Herzog and de Meuron Museum on the other: Tate Modern. Obviously the director, Serota, is of that whole white-box tendency, and it's easy to understand why – I mean, I can see a lot of good arguments why the container should never upstage the content, or should never even begin to think it is as important as the content. Gehry showed a different way, where people now discuss the Bilbao Museum rather than the Richard Serra that's inside it. But really I don't think it's only one or the other, and I don't think I have to join in either of those camps.

Collings

Were you conscious early on of curves as an identifying thing, a brand for you? Or did you only realize after a while that they'd become that?

Arad

It was never a manifesto. You can only ever post-rationalize. And you feature your weaknesses and you…

Collings

…make something positive out of your weaknesses?

Arad

Yes – because although I'd certainly spent a lot of time drawing, I wasn't a patient draughtsman. And I was never going to spread the tools on the table and do all that patient plotting, and so on. So I navigated through to areas that I'm better at. To make a manifesto out of it would be silly. But to recognize that that's what you do, well, that's fine.

Collings

But your chairs and tables and shelves and other objects all seem to – wherever else they might go – they all seem to want to go back to being

3-Skin Joint
Chair
2002
Composite materials, Nomex resin-impregnated paper
The Gallery Mourmans, 2002

'A chair made of three curved skins bonded together. The geometry of the skins provides the strength of this extremely lightweight piece.'

BOOP coffee table

1999
Polished superplastic aluminium
Ron Arad Studio and The Gallery Mourmans

'The BOOP (Blown Out Of Proportion)
collection comes entirely from the discovery
that you can inflate aluminium at high
temperature through robust steel stencils. It
was important to do pieces as big as the raw
aluminium sheets allowed to make clear there
was no other production technique that could
achieve these results. The coffee table, shown
here, is viewed from above.'

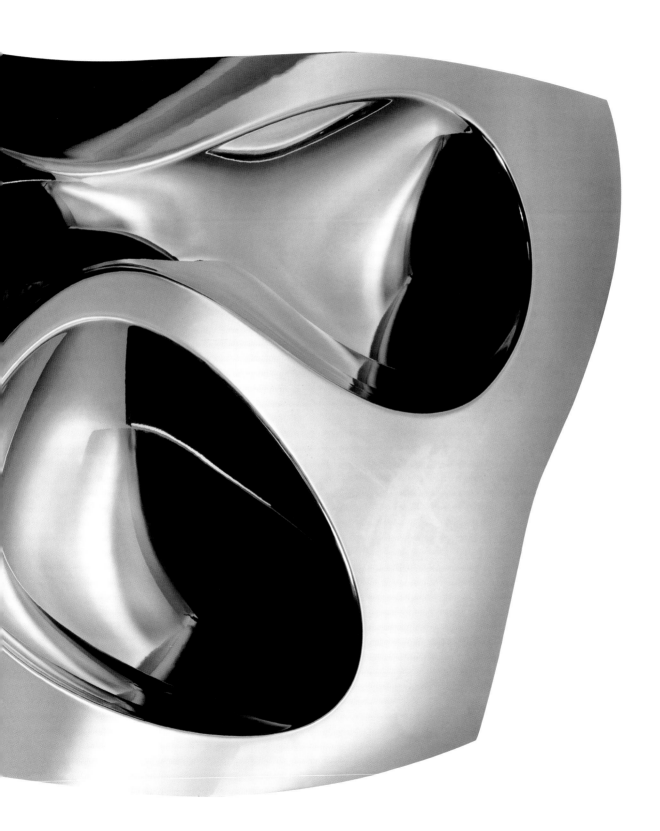

Looploom
Daybed
1992
Woven stainless steel, mirror-polished
stainless steel
Edition of 5
One Off Ltd

'A volume piece made not only of plates of steel,
but also a continuous loop of woven steel that
allows the piece to "sag" – as well as to have a
natural stability.'

Why curve?

a flamboyant thick pencil-mark line-curve. They seem to want to go back to something organic. Not organic like Arshile Gorky – more *The Flintstones*, more humorous-organic.

Arad

Right, yes – I mean, if this is a question, then I'd answer, 'Yes': it's there, freedom from the tyranny of the straight line and the orthogonal space and the ninety degrees. Also, there was an ugly period in brutalist architecture, where the ninety degrees were always chopped and truncated to forty-five degrees to make the building more interesting.

Collings

You mean, freedom from variations on angular-geometric?

Arad

Yes. But the thing is like in psychotherapy when they have a way of measuring the success of a treatment, and some people spend their life doing researches like this. And the biggest consideration wasn't whether it was a Jungian or a Freudian or a Kleinian or whatever discipline that was followed. It was something else. I think it's the same in our profession: you can be a fantastic minimalist architect and you can do fantastic things with straight lines. Or if you're Gehry you can do wonky walls – I wouldn't say you can do a postmodern building, because I don't think just anyone can. Maybe in this case one could argue the point and offer some examples – and you could find that in spite of the stable it comes from, the building has some quality. But yes, I do appreciate the need to sort things out and to categorise things. But I think it's really up to other people to do that – it's not so much up to the people who are categorized. I mean, Daniel Libeskind starts from a very funny point: you know – how do you translate the Holocaust into a building? I could never begin to do it. And in the end the whole thing is only like a big Rorschach test anyway: there are the marks and now you make sense of them.

Collings

To make a final comparison with art – it's striking that in art at the moment there are very few examples that one can think of where the sign of the artist is something that has a visual flourish: instead it's usually an idea-quirk, or a borrowed imagery-quirk.

Arad

Well, I think if you look at most artists whose names you know, you can easily say what their work looks like. You immediately think of the colours of Gilbert and George, say.

Collings

I can see what identifies their work, and it isn't a single visual thing exactly, it's a whole set of poses. And I can't think of a lot of current artists whose identifying trademark is anything strikingly visual. Or that has some kind of visual flourish to it. Or has something visually energetic.

Arad

This all goes into your new theory that Fine Art-type art isn't visual anymore, doesn't it?

Collings

Yeah. It's visual but only in a narrow and repetitive way, a sort of see-how-dumb-I-am grid-like way, or essentially referring-to-Minimalism way.

Arad

Yes, so you can force anything to fit, yes. But, having said that I do believe that artists do have a look, they do have something they can't help. Because the biggest source of raw material that you have when you work isn't magazines and books and previous art, it's really your own previous work. When you work you choose to do something one way, and there are lots of other ways you could have done it, but you just think, well, maybe next time. And then later you do actually come back to it. You talked about that JG Ballard book earlier. But his last one is really the same as the one before. I mean – it's the same but better. The same structure, the same beginning, the same…Did we talk enough? Did we curve enough, do you think?

Collings

Yes, that was good curving.

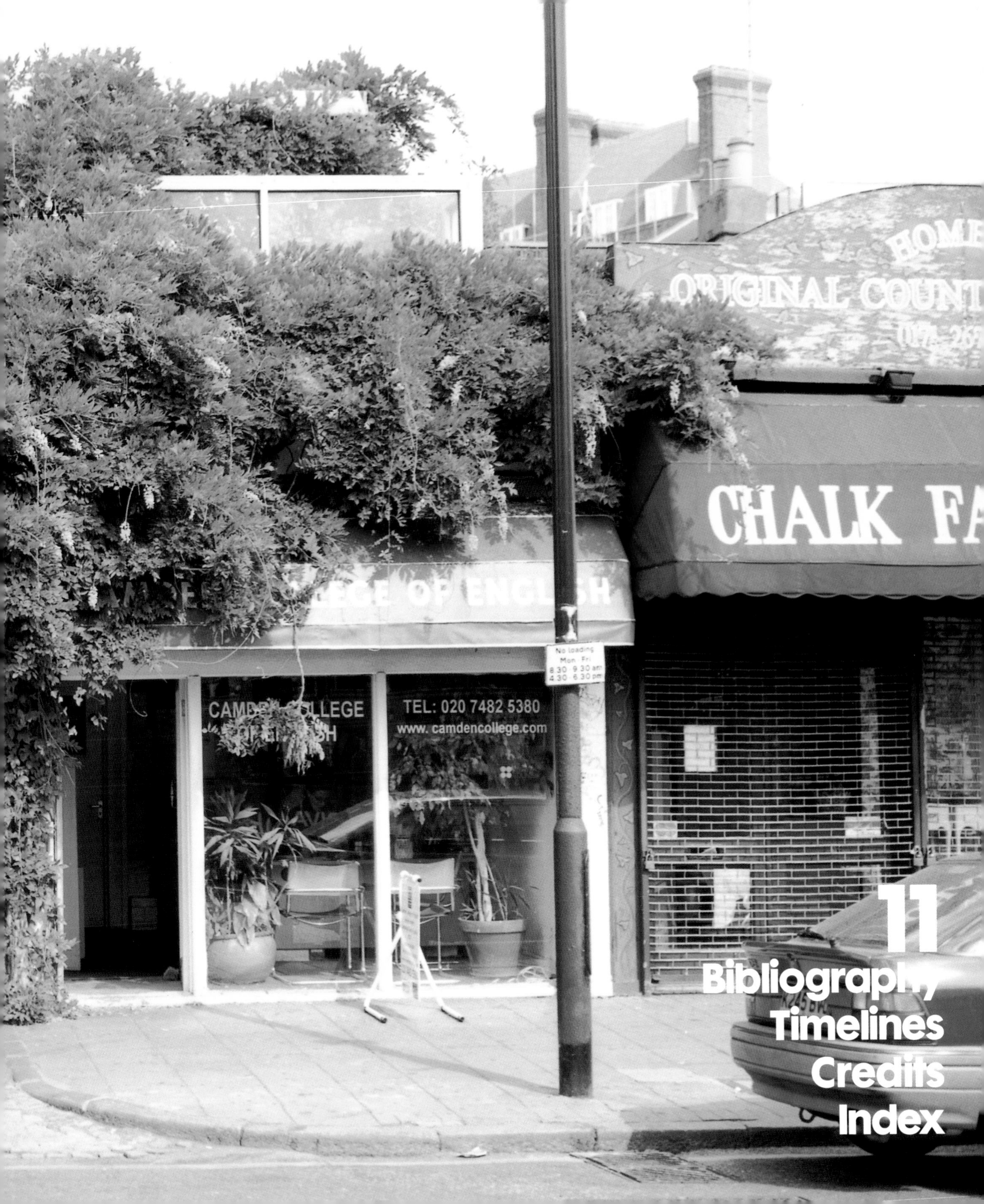

11 Bibliography Timelines Credits Index

Selected articles and essays

Elzbieta Wrzecionkowdka, 'Still more to be done', *The Warsaw Voice*, 18 December 1994

Deyan Sudjic, 'Evolution of the metal man', *Independent on Sunday*, 8 June 1997

Helen Greenwood, 'Shaper of Things to Come', *Sunday Morning Herald* (Sydney), 26 July 1997

Ali Gripper, 'Iconoclast designer with lots of shelf life', *Sunday Morning Herald* (Sydney), 11 August 1997

Rowan Moore, 'Let's give the coffee table genius a crack at the big stuff', *Evening Standard*, 8 September 1998

Nonie Niesewand, 'What do my creations actually do? Who cares?', *The Independent*, 11 September 1998

Lesley Gillilan, 'Well tempered rooms', *The Independent on Sunday*, 23 May 1999

Marcus Field, 'Ron Arad is looking happy', *Blueprint*, December 1999

Deyan Sudjic, 'Winwand', *Art & Events – Canary Wharf*, 2000

Lesley Gillilan, 'Pipe dreams', *The Guardian*, 27 January 2000

Alice Rawsthorn, 'Still making a splash', *Financial Times Weekend*, 17 June 2000

Deyan Sudjic, 'Pull up a car seat and make yourself at home', *The Observer*, 18 June 2002

Frances Stonor Saunders, 'Professor of cool', *New Statement*, 19 June 2000

Corinne Julius, 'Enter the mind of a Maverick', *Evening Standard*, 21 June 2000

Richard Dorment, 'V&A: Before & After– How was this disgrace allowed?', *Daily Telegraph*, 19 July 2000

Rowan Moore, 'How Ron caused a rumpus at the V&A', *Evening Standard*, 21 July 2000

'Exhibition of the week: Ron Arad, Victoria & Albert Museum', *The Week*, 5 August 2000

George H Marcus, 'Furniture with attitude', *Inside Magazine*, Autumn 2001

Ron Arad, 'Work that doesn't need to answer', *Looking Back in Envy: 20th Century Art and Design Revisited*, Jan Kaplicky (ed), John Wiley & Sons/Architectural Design, September 2001

François Delrieu, 'Around design with Ron Arad', *Environment & Composites*, n 9, October 2001

Alison Clements, 'Selfridges opts to be a leading light on display', *Retail Week*, 12 October 2001

Caroline Wingfield, 'Haute fidelity', *The Independent Magazine*, 3 November 2001

Zoe Ryan, 'Future shock', *Surface*, n 33, 2002

Jonathan Glancey, 'A name to conjure with', *Intra*, March 2002

Walter Ellis, 'Storm over "visual rape" at the V&A', *Independent on Sunday*, 23 July 2002

'Destroy all categories: Ron Arad', *Building*, 6 July 2003

Vinny Lee, 'Rebel, rebel', *The Times Magazine*, 6 September 2003

Books

Deyan Sudjic, *Restless Furniture*, Fourth Estate, 1989

Alexander von Vegesack, *Ron Arad*, Vitra, 1990

Ron Arad Associates: One Off Three (with essay by Volker Albus and introductions by Ettore Sottsass and Cedric Price), Artemis Architectural Publications, 1993

Volker Albus, *Design Classics: Bookworm*, Form Verlag, 1997

Raymond Guidot and Olivier Boissière, *Ron Arad*, Editions Dis Voir, 1998

Deyan Sudjic, *Ron Arad*, Laurence King, 1999

Exhibitions and awards

1986
'Intellectual Interiors', Seibo, Tokyo
(with Philippe Starck, Rei Kawakubo and
Shiro Kuramata)

1987
'Documenta 8', Kassel, Germany

'Nouvelles Tendences', Centre Georges
Pompidou, Paris

'Ron Arad Recent Works', Tel Aviv Museum of
Art, Israel

'Sticks and Stones', Vitra Design Museum
touring exhibition (until 1995)

1991
'A Break with Tradition', Rohska Museum,
Gothenburg, Sweden

1993
'Breeding in Captivity', Edward Totah
Gallery, London

'Design in the 20th Century', Grand Palais, Paris

'One Off and Short Runs', Centre for
Contemporary Arts, Warsaw-Krakow-Prague

1994
Designer of the Year, Salon du Meuble, Paris

'L'Espirit du Nomade', Fondation Cartier, Paris

1995
'Ron Arad and Ingo Maurer', Triennale, Milan

'The Work of Ron Arad', Museum of Applied
Arts, Helsinki

'Ron Arad', Gazi, Athens

1996
'Ron Arad and Ingo Maurer', Spazio Krizia, Milan

Glasgow Festival of Architecture & Design

1997
'Ron Arad', The Powerhouse Museum,
Sydney, Australia

'Ron Arad: New Acquisitions', Montreal
Museum of Decorative Arts

'Ron Arad and Ingo Maurer', Spazio Krizia, Milan

1998
'R.T.W', Gallery of Modern Art, Glasgow

'Ron Arad and Ingo Maurer', Spazio Krizia, Milan

1999
Wins competition to design a new range of
packaging for Fed-Ex, Germany

Design Plus Award, Frankfurt/Main

Internationlaer Designpreis Baden-
Wurttemberg, Design Center, Stuttgart

2000
'Before and After Now', Victoria & Albert
Museum, London

'Not Made by Hand, Not Made in China',
Galeria Marconi, Milan

2001
Oribe Art & Design Award, Gifu, Japan

Gio Ponti International Design Award, Denver

Barcelona Primavera International Award
for Design

Co-winner of Perrier Jouet Selfridges Design
Prize, London

'Delight in Dedark', Galeria Marconi, Milan

2002
Made a Royal Designer for Industry (RDI)

Made a Fellow of the World Technology Network

'Two Floors', Galeria Marconi, Milan

2003
Topot pots/planters win New York's ICFF
Press Award

'Permetre's La Libertat', Centre d'Art Santa
Monica, Barcelona

'Ron Arad', Galeria Marconi, Milan

'Von Mensch zu Mensch', Sparda Bank, Munster

'Ron Arad Studio Works: 1981–2003', Louisa
Guinness Gallery, London

'Ron Arad in der Galerie Stefan Vodgt', Galerie
der Moderne, Munich

2004
A&W (Architektur & Wohnen) magazine
Designer of the Year 2004 Award

'Lo-rez-dolores-tabula-rasa, Galeria
Marconi, Milan

Architectural projects, sculptures and installations

1983
Studio for One Off, Neal Street, Covent Garden, London

Bazaar, fashion outlet for Jean-Paul Gaultier, London

1985
A New Descending Staircase, Studio/showroom in Neal Street, London

1986
Furniture showroom for One off, Shelton Street, Covent Garden, London

1990
Milano Monamour, fashion outlet in Via della Spiga, Milan

Equation, department store for London fashion designers, Bristol

Camomilla, fashion outlet in historic building in Piazza de Spagna, Rome

The Bureau, conversion of warehouse in Wapping into design studios, London

Philips Electronic Exhibition, exhibition design incorporating Philips technology, Berlin

1991
Ron Arad Associates Studios, conversion of warehouse in Chalk Farm into a gallery, architecture studio and workshops, London (collaborator: Alison Brooks)

1993
Salon du Meuble de Paris Competition, exhibition design for the focus area of the Paris Furniture Fair

Publishing Studio, hillside building in Schopfheim in the Black Forest, Germany

1994
Michelle Mabelle, refurbishment of fashion outlet in the Via della Spiga, Milan

Belgo Noord, extension incorporating a new roof, bar, seating area, food preparation areas and a public beer store, London (collaborator: Alison Brooks)

The New Tel Aviv Opera House, freeform concrete structure within Opera complex, incorporating a restaurant, 5 bars, box office, bookshop, amphitheatre and mezzanine, Israel (collaborator: Alison Brooks)

1995
Office 'Y' Building, scheme for an international headquarters (in conjunction with David Chipperfield Architects), Seoul

Belgo Centraal, conversion of a warehouse in Covent Garden into a restaurant and head office, London (collaborators: Monique van den Hurk, Alison Brooks)

Galerie Achenbach, art gallery with pivoting walls that allow an infinite number of room layouts, Dusseldorf

1996
Adidas Stadium, winning scheme for a flagship complex for Adidas, Paris

Adidas/Kronenbourg Sports Cafés, development of a concept for bar/restaurants equipped with interactive audio-visual technology, France (Adidas collaborator: Shaun Fernandes)

British Room at the Louisiana Museum of Modern Art, concept and layout for section of the 'Design and Identity' exhibition, Denmark

Stand for Mercedes Benz AG, proposal for travelling internet stand to be used at the Birmingham Motor Show, Birmingham

1997
Haverstock Hill, conversion of the top floors of a Victorian house into an open-plan and partially open-air space, London

14–15 Conduit Street, scheme for a reception area in a newly refurbished office building, London

Private Residence, spatial elements and furniture for a newly-built villa, Israel

Domus Totem, commissioned by Domus magazine for the centre of the city: a sculpture made from a stack of 100 chairs in vacuum-formed aluminium, Milan

Gallery for Science Museum, short-listed competition scheme for the 'Making the Modern World' gallery, London

Private Residence (The Amiga House), project for a house on an acre of land in a suburban street, based on the overlap of two sheltering enclosures, London (collaborators: Barnaby Gunning, Geoff Crowther)

1998
The Piper Project, loft conversion featuring a mezzanine 'hull' designed to create a second level, London (collaborator: Geoff Crowther)

Windwand, 50-metre tapering mast that oscillates in the wind, topped by an illuminated section packed with LEDs, London

1999
Staircase for Tods, mirrored stainless steel staircase split into an upper canopy and lower stair ramp, Italy

Alan Journo Shop, extension of a small retail space into the basement, using a grand spiralling staircase, Milan

Exhibition for Glasgow 1999, exhibition design for 'Glasgow Winning: The Design of Sport' for Glasgow 1999, UK City of Architecture and Design (collaborators: Barnaby Gunning, Geoff Crowther)

The Big Blue, large circular sculpture in the centre of Canada Square Park, London

2001
Selfridges Technology Floor, design for new floor of the department store that features over 80 high-tech brands, London (collaborators: Geoff Crowther, Asa Bruno)

Tim, concept design for Tim Shops, Italy

Selfridges Christmas windows, display on Oxford Street featuring product ranges lit to create giant scrolling messages, London

(ongoing) Sheikh Saud Al-Thani Millennium House, design for living room and dining room of domestic residence in Doha, featuring a programmable floor and lighting system, Qatar (collaborator: Geoff Crowther)

2002
GrandHotelSalone, design for a hotel room exhibited at the Salone Internazionale del Mobile, Milan (collaborator: Asa Bruno)

Design products

Wonderwall for Manchester Stadium, proposal for a public art piece: a solid stainless steel wall made from 600 dynamic computer-controlled piston pixels

2003

Evergreen!, a bench/planter/pergola sculpture in the form of an infinity sign, placed outside the Mori Building in Roppongi, Tokyo (collaborator: Yukiko Tango)

Showroom for Maserati Headquarters, flagship showroom in Modena, Italy (collaborators: Geoff Crowther, Asa Bruno)

Cultural Festival Exhibition, exhibition enclosure for a display of Islamic Art in Dohar, Qatar (collaborators: Egon Hansen, Asa Bruno, Geoff Crowther)

Vallarta Tower, competition entry for a 30-storey building in Guadalajara that incorporates a vertical parking facility, Mexico (collaborator: Geoff Crowther)

Y's Store, flagship store for Yohji Yamamoto in the Roppongi Hills development, Tokyo (collaborator: Asa Bruno)

Ongoing

Hotel Duomo, refurbishment of a hotel in Rimini, Italy (collaborators: Geoff Crowther, Julian Gilhespie)

Hotel Puerta America, commission to design 30 rooms in a new-build hotel project, Madrid (collaborator: Egon Hansen)

Upperworld Hotel, commission to design a 50-bedroom hotel at roof level in Battersea Power Station, London (collaborators: Geoff Crowther, Nicola Hawkins, Asa Bruno, James Foster, Egon Hansen, Paul Gibbons)

1981
'Rover Chair' (One Off)
'Aerial Light' (One Off)
'The Transformer', chair (One Off)
'Round Railed Bed' (One Off)

1983
'Concrete Stereo' (One Off)

1985
'Horn', chairs (One Off)
'Platform C', cantelevered platform bed and wardrobe (One Off)

1986
'Shadow of Time', light/projected clock (One Off/Ron Arad Associates)
'Cone', tables and chair (One Off)
'Full House', chairs (One Off)
'Well Tempered Chair' (Vitra Editions)

1987
'The School Chair' (Vitra)

1988
'Big Easy' chair, 'Rolling Volume' chair and 'Italian Fish', Volumes series (One Off/Ron Arad Associates)
'Tinker Chair' (One Off)

1989
'Little Heavy', chair (One Off/Ron Arad Associates)
'Looming Lloyd', chair (One Off/Ron Arad Associates)
'Chair By Its Cover' (One Off)
'Why Bark? Why Dog?', chair (One Off/Ron Arad Associates)
'Reflection on Another Chair', series (One Off/Ron Arad Associates)
'Schizzo', chair (Vitra)
'Split', table (Poltronova)
'Big Easy 2 for 2', sofa (Ron Arad Associates)
'Rolling Volume', chair (One Off)

1990
'Spanish Made', chair (One Off/Ron Arad Associates)
'Beware of the Dog', daybed (Vitra)
'Old Dog New Tricks', seating (Vitra)
'Let Sleeping Dogs, Sit', seating (Vitra)
'The Spring Collection', 12 chairs/ sofas (Moroso)
'Soft Big Easy', chair (Moroso)
'Soft Heart', chair (Moroso)
'Sit', chair (One Off/The Gallery Mourmans)

1991
'Eight By One', chair (One Off/Ron Arad Associates)
'90° In The Shade', table (One Off)
Desk-top accessories (Lippert Wilkins)
'AYOR', chair (One Off/The Gallery Mourmans)

1992
'After Spring', daybed (One Off/Ron Arad Associates)
'2Rnot', chair (One Off/Ron Arad Associates)
'London Parpadelle', chair (One Off/Ron Arad Associates)
'Hotel Zeus', TV and video stand (Noto)
'Looploop', chair (One Off)
'Looploom', daybed (One Off)
'Large Bookworm', flexible shelving (One Off)

1993
'This Mortal Coil', bookcase (One Off/Ron Arad Associates)
'One Way or Another', bookcase (One Off/Ron Arad Associates)
'Bookworm', bookcase (Kartell)
'Misfits', modular seating system (Moroso)
'Zigo' and 'Zago', chairs (Driade)
'The Empty Chair' (Driade)
'T44 trolley' (Driade)
'Fly Ply', table (Driade)

1994
'Fly on the Wall', shelving system (One Off/Ron Arad Associates)
'Box in Four Movements', chair (Ron Arad Studio)
'And The Rabbit Speaks', chair (One Off/Ron Arad Associates)
'A Suitable Case', case/chair (One Off/Ron Arad Associates)
'D-Sofa' (One Off)
'Sof-Sof', seating system (Moroso)
'Anonymous' range, stools, chairs and tables for café use (Noto)
Plastic version of 'Bookworm' that comes coiled in a box (Kartell)
'Cartier Table' (Ron Arad Studio)

1995
'Sof-Sof', seating system (Moroso)
'Cler', shelving/display system (Fiam)
'38 Tables' (Ron Arad Associates)

1996
'Cross Yours T's', chair (Mercedes)
'RTW: Reinventing the Wheel', rollable
shelving system (Ron Arad Associates)
Double-skinned toilet (Allia)
'Half a Dozen', egg holder (Glaskoch)
Brandy flask, (Martell)

1997
'FPE: Fantastic Plastic Elastic Chair' (Kartell)
'Tom Vac', chair – a version of the Ron Arad
Studio vacuum-formed aluminium chair (Vitra)
'Carbo Tom', chair (Ron Arad Associates)
'Pic Chairs' (Ron Arad Associates)
'Un-cut', chair (Ron Arad Associates)
'H&H', shelving system (Kartell)

1998
'BOOP: Blown out of Proportion' collection,
one-off coffee tables and vases (The
Gallery Mourmans)
'The Soundtrack', CD storage system (Alessi)
'Infinity Winerack' (Kartell)
'Memo', bean-bag (Inflate)
Carbon-fibre daybed (Vitra)
Version of 'Tom Vac' chair in
injection-moulded plastic (Vitra)

1999
Variations on 'Tom Vac' chair, including
'Tom Rock', rocking chair (Vitra)
Double-skinned Champagne Glass (Glaskoch)
'Duemila', door handle (Valli & Valli)
'Rotolo', wireless speaker (NAC)
'New Orleans', armchair – a version of 'The Big
Easy' chair (The Gallery Mourmans)
'The Table That Eats Chairs', table and
chairs (Cassina)
'Konx Table' (Fiam)
'Movie', vases (The Gallery Mourmans)
'Stereolithography', vases (The
Gallery Mourmans)
'Vases' (The Gallery Mourmans)

2000
'Not Made by Hand, Not made in China'
range, vases, lamps and bowls (The Gallery
Mourmans) (collaborators: Geoff Crowther,
Yukiko Tango)
'No Waste Table' (Hidden)
'Victoria & Albert' range, chairs and sofas
(Moroso) (collaborator: Yukiko Tango)
Version of the 'RTW' rollable shelving system
in aluminium (Hidden)
'Little Albert', chair (Moroso)

2001
Snack bowls based on themes of 'Baby BOOP'
series (Alessi)
'Delight in Dedark', interactive curtain
(The Gallery Mourmans)
'IPCOs: Inverted Pinhole Camera Obscuras',
light (The Gallery Mourmans)
'Ballpark', rubberised mirrored grids
(Ingo Maurer GmbH) 'Plastic Little Albert' –
a rotation-moulded version of the small
'Victoria & Albert' chair (Moroso)
'Carbon Little Heavy', chair (The
Gallery Mourmans)
(work in progress) 'Swan Chair' (Magis)
(collaborator: Yuko Tsurumaru)
'Ge-Off Sphere', light (The Gallery Mourmans)
'Perfect' and 'Bouncing Vases' (The
Gallery Mourmans)
'Hot Ingo' and 'Hot Tango', lights (The
Gallery Mourmans)

2002
'Baby BOOPs', vase based on themes of 'BOOP'
series (Alessi)
'None Rota' and 'Nino Rota', chairs (Cappellini)
(collaborator: Yukiko Tango)
'Nina Rota', bed (Cappellini)
(collaborator: Yukiko Tango)
'Marilor Table', coffee table (Fiam)
'Paperwork' range, including a rocking chaise
longue, a rocking chair, dining chairs, a table
and a desk (The Gallery Mourmans)
(collaborator: Yukiko Tango)
Indoor/outdoor dining and coffee
tables (Moroso)
'Topot', outdoor plant pot (Serralunga)
(collaborator: Yukiko Tango)
'Bad Tempered Chair' – carbon-fibre version of
the 'Well Tempered Chair' (Vitra)
'3-Skin Joint', chair (The Gallery Mourmans)

2003
'Ron-alda', sofa (Bonaldo)
'Ron-aldo Down', lounge chair (Bonaldo)
(collaborator: Yuko Tsurumaru)
'Ron-aldo UP', dining chair (Bonaldo)
(collaborator: Yuko Tsurumaru)
'S.O.S.: Sort of Shelves', shelving system (Magis)
(collaborator: Marcus Hirst)
'Voido', rocking chair (Magis) (collaborator:
Yukiko Tango)
'The Big E' – a rotation-moulded version of the
'Big Easy' (Moroso)

2004
'Chiringuito', cocktail range (Alessi)
(collaborator: Yukiko Tango)

Companies by country
Italy: Kartell, Magis, Noto, NAC, Moroso, Valli &
Valli, Driade, Fiam, Cappellini, Alessi, Cassina,
Bonaldo, Serralunga

Germany: Glaskoch, Ingo Maurer GmbH

France: Martell

Switzerland: Vitra

Belgium: The Gallery Mourmans

UK: Inflate

The business

1981
Ron Arad and Caroline Thorman establish One Off, a design studio, workshops and showroom in Covent Garden, London

1989
Ron Arad and Caroline Thorman establish Ron Arad Associates, an architecture and design practice in Chalk Farm, London

1993
One Off is incorporated into Ron Arad Associates

1994
The Ron Arad Studio is established in Como, Italy to continue and expand on the production studio pieces previously produced in the London workshops (closes in 1994)

Ron Arad Associates current team
Ron Arad, Caroline Thorman (directors)

Architecture: Geoff Crowther (associate architect), Asa Bruno, Egon Hansen, Nicky Hawkins, Julian Gilhespie, James Foster, Taichi Kanemura

Design: Yukiko Tango (associate designer), Yuko Tsurumaru, Marcus Hirst, Helena Ambrosio

Administration: Pascale Gibon

Computer Generated Imaging: Paul Gibbons

Thanks

Ron Arad and Caroline Thorman would like to thank:

The Ron Arad Associates team for computer imaging.

Matthew Collings for his conversation.

3D Systems, England, for producing the stereolithography object for the cover.

Ernest Mourmans for hosting and facilitating the photography sessions.

Emilia Terragni at Phaidon for coordinating and overseeing production of this book.

Ally Ireson for text quality control.

Photographic credits

Specially commissioned photography
Richard Davies: pages 176–7
Graphic Thought Facility: jacket and pages 2–3
Nigel Shafran: pages 6–7, 20–1, 36–7, 54–5, 68–9, 78–9, 108–9, 162–3, 184–5, 220–1, 236–7
Tom Vack: pages 8, 18, 66, 80, 90–3, 96–7, 99, 100, 102, 104–5, 122–3, 132–5, 138–9, 147–9, 156–61, 222, 229–33.

Archive photography
Alessandro from Udine, Grisha Arad, Ron Arad, Asa Bruno, Gadi Dagon, Richard Davies, Christoph Kicherer, Howard Kingsnorth, Mamoru Miyajima, Wilhelm Moser, Nacasa & Partners, Yukiko Tango, Caroline Thorman, Tom Vack and Ian Whittaker.

Reference images
The following images have been supplied courtesy of: Richard Artschwager and Mary Boone Gallery, page 9; Max Protetch Gallery, page 10 top; Louisa Guinness Gallery, page 10 bottom (photograph by Deborah Denker); Vitra, page 11 top; Fritz Hansen, page 11 bottom; Phillips, page 13; Cassina, page 16; Liam Gillick, page 19 top, Peter halley, page 19 bottom; Bernard Tschumi, page 26; Mark Fisher, page 27; Peter Cook, page 29, Phillips, page 60 left; Jeff Koons, page 72; Franz West, page 86; Victoria & Albert Museum, page 178 bottom; Citroën, page 204; Arata Isozaki, page 227.

Jacket and pages 2–3 show 'Stereolithographies' model of Ron Arad and Matthew Collings' signatures designed by Ron Arad, modelled by Paul Gibbons. Jacket concept by Graphic Thought Facility.

Index

Figures in italics indicate captions.

Phaidon Press
Regent's Wharf
All Saints Street
London N1 9PA

Phaidon Press Inc.
180 Varick Street
New York, NY 10014

www.phaidon.com

First Published 2004
© 2004 Phaidon Press Limited

ISBN 0 7148 4310 5

Designed by Graphic Thought Facility
Printed in Hong Kong